PREVENTING WASTE, FRAUD, ABUSE, AND MISMANAGEMENT IN HOMELAND SECURITY— A GAO HIGH-RISK LIST REVIEW

HEARING

BEFORE THE

COMMITTEE ON HOMELAND SECURITY
HOUSE OF REPRESENTATIVES

ONE HUNDRED THIRTEENTH CONGRESS

SECOND SESSION

MAY 7, 2014

Serial No. 113–67

Printed for the use of the Committee on Homeland Security

Available via the World Wide Web: http://www.gpo.gov/fdsys/

U.S. GOVERNMENT PRINTING OFFICE

89–762 PDF   WASHINGTON : 2014

(II)

CONTENTS

PREVENTING WASTE, FRAUD, ABUSE, AND MISMANAGEMENT IN HOMELAND SECURITY—A GAO HIGH-RISK LIST REVIEW

Wednesday, May 7, 2014

U.S. HOUSE OF REPRESENTATIVES,
COMMITTEE ON HOMELAND SECURITY,
Washington, DC.

The committee met, pursuant to call, at 10:09 a.m., in Room 311, Cannon House Office Building, Hon. Michael T. McCaul [Chairman of the committee] presiding.

Present: Representatives McCaul, Broun, Duncan, Hudson, Sanford, Thompson, Clarke, Richmond, Payne, and O'Rourke.

Chairman MCCAUL. Committee on Homeland Security will come to order. Committee is meeting today to examine testimony regarding the prevention of waste, fraud, abuse, and mismanagement at the Department of Homeland Security. I recognize myself for an opening statement.

While the Department of Homeland Security's mission is critical, it is also critical that it keeps its finances in check because in order to protect the homeland we must maximize every dollar spent. Almost as soon as the Department's creation, the Government Accountability Office placed some of DHS's programs on its high-risk list, and today many remain.

This list is developed every 2 years by watchdogs at GAO to identify areas in the Federal Government that are high-risk to fraud, waste, abuse, and mismanagement, or are in the most need of broad reform. It is intended to draw attention to these areas to force agency leaders to improve.

Unfortunately some of the programs identified include some of the Department's core functions such as acquisitions, management, financial management, information technology, human capital and management integration, as well as multi-agency challenges such as information sharing and cybersecurity.

While the Department has devoted time to addressing GAO's high-risk areas, these reports continue to show examples of programs ignoring best practices and putting taxpayer dollars at risk.

Recent GAO findings have identified challenges with the Arizona Border Surveillance Technology Plan, TSA body scanners, modernization of key border enforcement system known as TECS, and the Department's acquisition funding plans.

All levels of DHS must be fully committed to make the Department more efficient and effective. To this end, this committee has taken action to address specific issues highlighted in GAO's high-risk report.

H.R. 3696, the National Cybersecurity and Critical Infrastructure Protection Act, and H.R. 4228, the DHS Acquisition Accountability and Efficiency Act both passed out of this committee unanimously and are important pieces of legislation to increase our Nation's cybersecurity and improve the Department's management of its acquisition programs.

Additionally, our recent bipartisan report on the Boston bombings highlighted the need for improved information sharing, which addresses another high-risk item.

Finally, while I am encouraged by the steps taken by DHS in recent years to address these issues, including achieving a clean audit opinion in 2013, there is clearly much more work to be done. In the short time since they have assumed their new positions, Secretary Johnson and Deputy Secretary Mayorkas have both already endeavored to fix the management problems at DHS. Today I look forward to hearing from them on their plans to improve the Department.

However, assurances from the top and putting plans in place only go so far. It will take time and follow-up and continued oversight to ensure improved outcomes are sustained over multiple years. To that end I look forward to Comptroller General Dodaro and recently-confirmed DHS Inspector General Roth's testimony today. Their recommendations to make DHS a more effective and efficient organization are essential to making Americans safer.

Ultimately every dollar wasted on mismanagement is one less that can go to the men and women protecting our borders, targeting terrorists, securing our airports, and patrolling our shores. That is why this hearing and DHS's commitment to getting its house in order is so important.

[The statement of Chairman McCaul follows:]

STATEMENT OF CHAIRMAN MICHAEL T. MCCAUL

MAY 7, 2014

While the Department of Homeland Security's mission is critical, it is also critical that it keeps its finances in check, because in order to protect the homeland we must maximize every dollar spent.

Almost as soon as the Department's creation, the Government Accountability Office (GAO) placed some of DHS's programs on its "High-Risk List," and today, many remain. This list is developed every 2 years by the watchdogs at GAO to identify areas in the Federal Government that are at high risk to fraud, waste, abuse, and mismanagement or are in most need of broad reform, and it is intended to draw attention to these areas to force agency leaders to improve.

Unfortunately, some of the programs identified include some of the Department's core functions such as acquisition management, financial management, information technology, human capital, and management integration, as well as, multi-agency challenges such as information sharing and cybersecurity.

While the Department has devoted time to addressing GAO's High-Risk areas, these reports continue to show examples of programs ignoring best practices and putting taxpayer dollars at risk. Recent GAO findings have identified challenges with the Arizona Border Surveillance Technology Plan, TSA body scanners, modernization of a key border enforcement system known as TECS, and the Department's acquisition funding plans. All levels of DHS must be fully committed to making the Department more efficient and effective.

To this end, this committee has taken action to address specific issues highlighted in GAO's High-Risk report. H.R. 3696, the National Cybersecurity and Critical Infrastructure Protection Act, and H.R. 4228, the DHS Acquisition Accountability and

Efficiency Act—both passed out of this committee unanimously—are important pieces of legislation to increase our Nation's cybersecurity and improve the Department's management of its acquisition programs. Additionally, our recent bipartisan report on the Boston bombings highlighted the need for improved information sharing, which addresses another High-Risk item.

Finally, while I am encouraged by the steps DHS has taken in recent years to address these issues including achieving a clean audit opinion in 2013, there is clearly much more work to be done. In the short time since they've assumed their new positions, Secretary Johnson and Deputy Secretary Mayorkas have both already endeavored to fix the management problems at DHS, and today I look forward to hearing more from them on his plan for improving the Department. However, assurances from the top and putting plans in place only go so far. It will take time and follow-up and continued oversight to ensure improved outcomes are sustained over multiple years.

To that end, I look forward to Comptroller General Dodaro and recently confirmed DHS Inspector General Roth's testimony today. Their recommendations to make DHS a more effective and efficient organization are essential to making Americans safer. Ultimately, every dollar wasted on mismanagement is one less that can go to the men and women protecting our borders, targeting terrorists, securing our airports, and patrolling our shores. That's why this hearing, and DHS' commitment to getting its house in order, is so important.

Chairman McCAUL. With that the Chairman now recognizes the Ranking Member, Mr. Thompson.

Mr. THOMPSON. Thank you, Mr. Chairman. I thank you for holding today's hearing. I also want to thank the comptroller general, deputy secretary, and inspector general for their testimonies today.

Today's hearing is to examine the Department of Homeland Security's management functions deemed high-risk by the Government Accountability Office, and the steps that the Department is taking to improve in these areas. At the beginning of each Congress the GAO releases its high-risk update, which focuses on agencies and programs that are vulnerable to waste, fraud, and abuse.

Understandably when the Department was formed in 2003 it was placed on the high-risk list because of the challenges associated on transforming 22 legacy agencies into one new Federal department. It was also put on the high-risk list because its failures to effectively do so could present National security risks.

Unfortunately, more than a decade after its inception the Department remains on the high-risk list. One reason is that the Department has struggled to integrate its management functions across all components. These integration challenges present diverse operational and management problems at the Department at all levels.

There has been general acceptance of the One DHS concept advanced by the last Secretary of Homeland Security. But what is needed at this pivotal moment is a leader who will animate that slogan and put structures and procedures in place to fully integrate the Department.

Secretary Johnson may well be that leader, but any reforms will be at the mercy of an entrenched and unhappy workforce and the clock. I look forward to working with Secretary Johnson to bring about needed reforms.

For the first time since its inception, however, the Department received its first clean audit of all its financial statements for fiscal year 2013. As commendable as this may be, we must not overlook that the independent auditor did find continued weaknesses in the Department's financial controls.

4

Another challenging area for the Department is its IT acquisitions and management. Over the years the Department has had varying success acquiring and implementing information technology systems. Some systems have performed as promised, while others have failed to deliver capabilities and mission benefit.

There is a need for the Department to strengthen its internal IT governance. GAO has noted that the Department has more work to do to fully address its IT management challenges such as finalizing policies and procedures associated with its new governance structure.

Finally, the Department spends approximately a quarter of its annual budget procuring goods and services in support of its homeland security missions. Yet since its inception, managing acquisitions has been a significant challenge for the Department.

The management framework put in place by the prior DHS leadership has the potential for improving DHS acquisition management in significant ways. That is why I am pleased that this committee was able to come together in a bipartisan fashion last week and pass H.R. 4228, the DHS Acquisition Accountability and Efficiency Act, which seeks to codify what has been deemed by the comptroller general and other watchdogs as successful, and seeks to close other gaps that exist.

Mr. Chairman, I look forward to more ways that this committee can work to help advance the Department and help it achieve the goals of being fully integrated with clean financial audits and internal management and oversight controls in its information technology and acquisition departments.

Given the pivotal role the Department has in protecting and preparing America, management challenges become a distraction and have grave consequences for our National security. Hence, it is my hope that the Department can continue to progress, and we can see a date when it is not a part of the GAO high-risk list.

With that, Mr. Chairman, I yield back. Thank you.

[The statement of Ranking Member Thompson follows:]

STATEMENT OF RANKING MEMBER BENNIE G. THOMPSON

MAY 7, 2014

Today's hearing is to examine the Department of Homeland Security's management functions deemed high-risk by the Government Accountability Office and the steps that the Department is taking to improve in these areas.

At the beginning of each Congress, the GAO releases its "High-Risk Update" which focuses on agencies and programs that are vulnerable to waste, fraud, and abuse. Understandably, when the Department was formed in 2003, it was placed on the "high-risk list" because of the challenges associated with transforming 22 legacy agencies into one new Federal Department. It was also put on the "high-risk list" because its failure to effectively do so could present National security risks.

Unfortunately, more than a decade after its inception, the Department remains on the "high-risk list." One reason is that the Department has struggled to integrate its management functions across all the components. These integration challenges present diverse operational and management problems at the Department at all levels.

There has been general acceptance of the "One DHS" concept advanced by the last Secretary of Homeland Security but what is needed at this pivotal moment is a leader who will animate that slogan and put structures and procedures in place to fully integrate the Department. Secretary Johnson may well be that leader but any reforms will be at the mercy of an entrenched and unhappy workforce and the clock. I look forward to working with Deputy Secretary Mayorkas and Secretary Johnson to bring about needed reforms.

For the first time since its inception, the Department received its first clean audit on all its financial statements for fiscal year 2013. As commendable as this may be, we must not overlook that the independent auditor did find continued weakness in the Department's financial controls.

Another challenging area for the Department is IT acquisitions and management. Over the years, the Department has had varying success acquiring and implementing information technology systems; some systems have performed as promised while others have failed to deliver capabilities and mission benefits. There is a need for the Department to strengthen its internal IT governance. GAO has noted that the Department has more work to do to fully address its IT management challenges such as finalizing policies and procedures associated with its new governance structure.

Finally, the Department spends approximately a quarter of its annual budget procuring goods and services in support of its homeland security missions. Yet, since its inception, managing acquisitions has been a significant challenge for the Department.

The management framework put in place by the Obama administration has the potential for improving DHS acquisitions management in significant ways. That is why I am pleased that this committee was able to come together in a bipartisan fashion last week and passed H.R. 4228, the "DHS Acquisition Accountability and Efficiency Act," which seeks to codify what has been deemed by the Comptroller General and other watchdogs as successful and seeks to close other gaps that exist.

I look forward to more ways that this committee can work to help advance the Department and help it achieve the goals of being fully integrated, with clean financial audits, and internal management and oversight controls in its information technology and acquisitions departments.

Given the pivotal role the Department has in protecting and preparing America, management challenges become a distraction and have grave consequences for our National security. Hence, it is my hope that the Department can continue to progress and we can see a day when it is not a part of the GAO High-Risk list.

Chairman McCAUL. I thank the Ranking Member. Other Members I remind they may submit an opening statement for the record.

We are pleased to have here today a distinguished panel of witnesses; first, the Honorable Alejandro Mayorkas, who was sworn in as deputy secretary of the Department of Homeland Security in December 2013.

Prior to his appointment he served as director of the Department's United States Citizenship and Immigration Services. He led a workforce of 18,000 employees throughout more than 250 offices world-wide rector of the Department's United States Citizenship and Immigration Services.

Before joining DHS Mr. Mayorkas was a partner at a law firm. In 1998 he was appointed as the United States Attorney for the Central District of California.

Thanks for being here today.

Next we have the Honorable Gene Dodaro, who became the eighth comptroller general of the United States, and head of the United States Government Accountability Office.

In December 2010, after serving in the capacity of "acting" since March 2008 as comptroller general he has helped oversee the development and issuance of hundreds of reports and testimonies each year to various committees and individual Members of Congress. These and other GAO products have led to hearings and legislation, billions of dollars in taxpayer savings, and improvements to a wide range of Government programs and services.

Then last but not least, the Honorable John Roth. Let me mention it is Mr. Dodaro's birthday today, and we wish you a happy birthday, as well.

Then last, Mr. John Roth, who assumed the post of inspector general for the Department of Homeland Security in March 2014. Previously he served as director of the Office of Criminal Investigations at the Food and Drug Administration. Prior to that, he had a long and distinguished record and career with the Department of Justice beginning in 1987 as Assistant U.S. Attorney for the Eastern District of Michigan.

It is great to see so many brethren DOJ on this panel. Their full written statements will appear on the record. The Chairman now recognizes Deputy Secretary Mayorkas for 5 minutes.

STATEMENT OF ALEJANDRO N. MAYORKAS, DEPUTY SECRETARY, U.S. DEPARTMENT OF HOMELAND SECURITY

Mr. MAYORKAS. Thank you very much, Mr. Chairman. Mr. Chairman and distinguished Members of this committee. I very much appreciate the opportunity to testify before you today. I feel privileged to appear before you as the deputy secretary of Homeland Security.

I pledged to this committee an open, transparent, and fully cooperative Department. We deeply appreciate the work of this committee and have profound respect for it. Strong oversight drives good Government, and we recognize and appreciate that.

I also want to thank my fellow witnesses before you today, Mr. Dodaro and Mr. Roth, for the work that they perform and that their teams perform. We share a common goal of making the Department everything that it should be.

Mr. Chairman, Ranking Member Thompson, and distinguished Members, I submitted to this committee written testimony, and I will not repeat it now.

I do want to underscore one overriding fact, and that is my immense pride in working alongside the men and women of the Department of Homeland Security. Those incredibly dedicated individuals deserve a Department and deserve management functions and processes and institutions that bring out the best in them and enable them to do their jobs at the highest levels of excellence to which they aspire.

With that I look forward to the opportunity to answer whatever questions you might have. Thank you.

[The prepared statement of Mr. Mayorkas follows:]

PREPARED STATEMENT OF ALEJANDRO N. MAYORKAS

MAY 7, 2014

Chairman McCaul, Ranking Member Thompson, and distinguished Members of the committee, thank you for the opportunity to appear before you as the deputy secretary of Homeland Security to testify on the subject of management at this important hearing entitled "Preventing Waste, Fraud, Abuse and Mismanagement in Homeland Security—a GAO High-Risk List Review." I, along with Secretary Johnson, appreciate and welcome the committee's continued focus on this subject and for the oversight you exercise. It is my firmly-held belief that good oversight not only delivers accountability critical to good government, but that it also drives innovation. Thank you, and thank you to the members of your staff.

I also wish to express my gratitude to the U.S. Government Accountability Office (GAO). Under Comptroller General Gene Dodaro's leadership, GAO has spent considerable time and energy providing our Department with its valued, independent assessment of our work in areas critical to the effective management of our resources and execution of our responsibilities. GAO has issued recommendations to our Department that, collectively, help provide a blueprint for success. It is in response to GAO's independent reviews and recommendations that in January 2011 our Department issued the first *Integrated Strategy for High Risk Management*, an operational framework to address GAO's recommendations. Since we issued the *Integrated Strategy*, we have updated it twice yearly to document the progress our Department has made in addressing GAO's recommendations. It pleases me to note that we have come far in the last 5 years; today the Department eagerly engages with GAO about outstanding recommendations. We seek out GAO.

Like the responsibility of the GAO to provide its independent assessment of the Department's execution of responsibilities, it is the duty of the Office of the Inspector General to deliver its own independent and high-quality review of Departmental functions. I am grateful to testify before you today alongside the Department's new inspector general, John Roth. I look forward to supporting the work of Inspector General Roth and to ensuring the Department's transparency and full cooperation as he and I work to improve and strengthen the Department in our respective roles.

When I became the deputy secretary of DHS in late December 2013, the first action I took was to schedule a meeting with Comptroller General Dodaro. In our meeting I had the opportunity to also meet George Scott, the managing director of GAO's Homeland Security and Justice team. Mr. Scott and I have met on several occasions since then, and he and his team are outstanding in their commitment to improving our Department. With Mr. Scott's and his team's independent efforts, with the oversight of GAO and that of this committee, DHS will mature and improve.

The number of open GAO recommendations to DHS has decreased steadily and, significantly, in GAO's latest High-Risk List update it narrowed the subject from "Implementing and Transforming DHS" to "Strengthening DHS Management Functions." Additionally noteworthy is the fact that GAO stated in that update that our Department's *Integrated Strategy*, "if implemented and sustained, provides a path for DHS to be removed from GAO's High-Risk List." DHS has made significant progress.

At the same time, DHS has additional work to do. Since I became the deputy secretary I have invested considerable time in working with GAO and with my very talented and dedicated DHS colleagues to ensure that this additional work is done as effectively and swiftly as possible. Earlier this year, we developed specific action plans to address the 30 key outcomes GAO identified in the areas of management integration, human capital, information technology, financial management, and acquisitions. Our action plans now provide month-to-month goals that provide a better road map to success. Our development of these action plans provided us with the opportunity to freshly review our previous efforts and, in certain critical areas, to accelerate our time tables materially.

STRENGTHENING DEPARTMENT OF HOMELAND SECURITY MANAGEMENT FUNCTIONS

Before discussing the work that DHS has undertaken to make progress on key GAO High-Risk List areas, I wish to highlight the actions we have recently taken that speak to our Departmental commitment to sound management practices. On April 22, 2014, the Secretary sent a memorandum to Department leadership entitled, "Strengthening Departmental Unity of Effort." The purpose of this effort is to capitalize on the many strengths of the Department, starting with the professionalism, skill, and dedication of its people and the rich history and tradition of its components, while identifying ways to enhance the cohesion of the Department as a whole. The Secretary's guidance is targeted at improvements to four main lines of effort: Inclusive senior leader discussion and decision-making forums that provide an environment of trust and transparency; strengthened fundamental and critical management processes for investment (including requirements, budget, and acquisition processes) that look at cross-cutting issues across the Department; focused, collaborative Departmental strategy, planning, and analytic capability that support more effective DHS-wide decision-making and operations; and, enhanced coordinated operations to harness the significant resources of the Department more effectively. Many of the elements of this effort are described below, as they cut across the several management areas discussed in GAO's High-Risk List.

GAO's High-Risk List focus on "Strengthening DHS Management Functions" identified the need to achieve progress in key management areas, including human capital management, financial management, acquisitions, information technology, and management integration. The Department's *Integrated Strategy for High-Risk Management* provides the framework for our efforts to address GAO's recommendations and integrate and strengthen our management infrastructure across the Department; our monthly action plans help ensure that we have goals and time lines to help us deliver success in timely fashion. I would like to share with you our efforts in each key area of focus.

Human Capital Management

The Department of Homeland Security's greatest asset is its dedicated and talented workforce. GAO has identified areas in which the Department must mature its human capital systems to ensure that its workforce is properly equipped and supported to achieve the Department's challenging missions. The Department, in turn, has accelerated time lines in its monthly action plans to achieve success in this critical area.

The low employee morale in several parts of the Department is an area of particular focus. Under the direction of Secretary Johnson, I am taking a series of steps to address the root causes of the low morale and to deliver for the workforce the Department it deserves. I have formed a steering committee comprised of personnel from each of the Department's component agencies and from Department headquarters to focus on, among other things, the following areas that the workforce has identified in the Federal Employee Viewpoint Survey and in other feedback vehicles as ones in which the Department can improve:

- *The hiring and promotion process.* DHS employees have expressed concerns that the hiring and promotion process is sometimes opaque. The Department can build greater employee confidence in the process through greater transparency and communication and by setting clear hiring and promotion standards.
- *Training and professional development.* DHS employees have expressed a desire for enhanced training opportunities to ensure they are equipped to perform their jobs at the highest levels of excellence. They also have sought professional development opportunities that will enable them to achieve the promotions or new opportunities to which they aspire.
- *Rewards and recognition.* DHS employees perform extraordinary acts of patriotism and courage each and every day throughout the Nation and the world. They deserve to be recognized, rewarded, and championed for their achievements. The Department is reintroducing the Secretary's annual awards to recognize outstanding individual and team achievements from across the Department. In addition, the Department will institutionalize the practice of regularly championing its workforce and rewarding them when appropriate.
- *Performance management.* Performance management is a critical tool in promoting priorities and values and driving accountability. The steering committee will focus on ensuring that each component and office in the Department has a performance management system that reflects the appropriate measures of success and drives each employee to achieve that success.

Financial Management

In fiscal year 2013, DHS achieved an historic unqualified clean audit opinion of all five financial statements, a confirmation of DHS's on-going commitment to sound financial management practices. This benchmark represented a huge accomplishment for the many DHS employees who work every day to increase transparency and accountability for the taxpayer resources entrusted to the Department. Americans have the right to expect that we will be responsible stewards of every homeland security dollar with which we are entrusted.

The Department expects to sustain this progress and receive its second clean audit opinion for fiscal year 2014. In the past 4 years, DHS has also eliminated 10 audit qualifications, reduced Department-wide material weaknesses in internal controls over financial reporting from 10 to 4, and significantly reduced the number of component conditions contributing to material weaknesses from 25 to 2. The Department is executing a multi-year plan to achieve an unqualified clean opinion for internal control of financial reporting by fiscal year 2016.

Financial system modernization is a priority area for the Department. DHS is executing specific modernization efforts in order to meet the Department's mission while minimizing and eliminating spending in duplicative systems. The current strategy conforms to guidance from the Office of Management and Budget to use shared services where possible and to split modernization projects into smaller, simpler segments with clear deliverables. One of our challenges in the shared services domain is that no one Federal agency has sufficient capacity to house all of the Department's financial management data. As a result, we are evaluating the capabilities of the Federal agencies who offer shared services arrangements. The DHS Chief Financial Officer has established enterprise-wide standards for each component to follow and has prioritized a deployment strategy based on those components with the highest business needs.

Acquisitions Management

The strategic decisions of the Department's senior leadership are only as good as the processes that support and give effect to those decisions in investments and in the conduct of operations. Historically, DHS has generally developed and executed component-centric requirements, which has resulted in inefficient use of limited resources. Much work has been done to date in the areas of joint requirements analysis, program and budget review, and acquisition oversight, including an effort over the past 4 years by the DHS Management Directorate to improve the Department's overall acquisitions process and reform even the earliest phase of the investment life cycle where requirements are first conceived and developed. The Secretary's April 22, 2014 memorandum on "Strengthening Departmental Unity of Effort" focuses and reinforces existing structures and creates new capability, where needed, as identified in the recent Integrated Investment Life Cycle Management (IILCM) pilot study and other process analyses that examined the linkages between these inter-related planning processes and operations. These analyses underscored the need to further strengthen all elements of the process, particularly the up-front development of strategy, planning, and joint requirements, and to ensure through collaborative, inclusive senior leadership dialogue and decision that they function in a way that considers DHS-wide missions and functions, rather than focusing on those of an individual component.

As an example, I am leading the Deputies Management Action Group in an expedited review to provide strategic alternatives for enhancing the current DHS joint requirements process. This review will include options for developing and facilitating a DHS component-driven, joint requirements process, including a program for oversight of a development test and evaluation capability, to identify priority gaps and overlaps in Departmental capability needs, provide feasible technical alternatives to meet capability needs, and recommend to me the creation of joint programs and joint acquisitions to meet Department-wide mission needs. This enhanced process will be used in expanding the mission portfolios studied in the IILCM pilot, which included Cybersecurity, Biodefense, and Screening and Vetting, to include Border Security and Air Domain.

DHS recently announced two important decisions that speak to our commitment to responsible and cost-effective acquisitions. First, DHS cancelled the BioWatch acquisition of autonomous detection technology (also known as Gen–3). Currently deployed in more than 30 metropolitan areas across the country, BioWatch provides public health officials with a warning of a biological agent release before potentially exposed individuals develop symptoms of illness. While autonomous detection is an important capability, the Gen–3 acquisition did not reflect the best use of resources in our current fiscal environment. DHS remains committed to the BioWatch program and will ensure that current BioWatch operations continue as part of our layered approach to biodefense. Second, DHS is putting on hold a FEMA Logistics Supply Chain Management System contract until further review. FEMA's Logistics Supply Chain Management System was developed to provide full disaster supply chain management capability and visibility to FEMA and its partners. The Department has determined that the program has not met all of its operational requirements and that it needs to be reviewed in the context of broader logistical operations. That review is underway, which will include a third-party evaluation of the most cost-effective manner. These decisions are in line with the Department's focus on efficiency, ensuring that we continue to pursue cost-effective acquisition without compromising our security. The Secretary and I will continue to hold our acquisition programs accountable to ensure they are responsible and cost-effective.

Additionally, the DHS Chief Financial Officer has strengthened and enhanced the Department's programming and budgeting process by incorporating the results of strategic analysis and joint requirements planning into portfolios for review by issue teams. Using this approach, substantive, large-scale alternative choices will be presented to the Deputies Management Action Group as part of the annual budget development. This review process will also include the Department's existing programmatic and budgetary structure, not just new investments. It will include the ability for DHS to project the impact of current decisions on resource issues such as staffing, capital acquisitions, operations and maintenance, and similar issues that impact the Department's future ability to fulfill its mission responsibilities. As its first task, the Deputies Management Action Group will focus this enhanced programming and budgeting process on the development of options for the fiscal year 2016 budget request.

In the oversight phase, we will continue to leverage the Component Acquisition Executive structure and enhanced business intelligence to proactively identify performance problems with existing programs throughout their life cycle. While there is work to be done to sustain our progress, we are encouraged by an Office of the

Inspector General report that stated that DHS has significantly strengthened our acquisition management oversight.

We have also made significant progress in strengthening the document review process. In 2013, the under secretary for management issued a decision memorandum stating that no new program can proceed without the approved acquisition documentation, including life-cycle cost estimates, mission needs statements, test and evaluation plans, and operational requirements documents.

To ensure we have an adequately staffed and trained acquisition workforce, the Department has engaged on multiple fronts to enhance acquisition staffing and training. The DHS Acquisition Professional Career Program (APCP) is sponsored by the chief procurement officer and provides a steady pipeline of entry-level contracting and procurement talent to the components. APCP interns are hired into career ladder positions and engage in a 3-year program where they receive quality training and rotate between components to gain valuable on-the-job training. In fiscal year 2013 alone, 63 interns graduated and have been placed in components. Thus far in fiscal year 2014, an additional 60 interns have been placed.

The Department's Homeland Security Acquisition Institute continues to serve as the principal training academy for the DHS acquisition workforce. In fiscal year 2013, over 9,400 DHS acquisition professionals completed classroom or on-line training courses contributing to the issuance of over 3,200 acquisition certifications. Thus far in fiscal year 2014, an additional 1,300 acquisition certifications have been issued. To date, DHS has issued 10,732 certifications across nine acquisition disciplines, including Contracting, Program Management, Systems Engineering, Test and Evaluation, Cost Estimating, Life Cycle Logistics Management, Program Financial Management, Ordering Official, and Contracting Officer's Representative.

DHS continues to support small businesses around the country. In recognition of its performance, the Department has received an "A" rating for 5 consecutive years from the Small Business Administration in the areas of prime contracting, small business subcontracting, and a written progress plan.

Information Technology Management

In the Information Technology (IT) area, DHS has made substantial progress to drive efficiencies through consolidation of data centers. To date, 18 primary data centers have been consolidated, with an additional two consolidations scheduled for completion in fiscal year 2014. Migrations from commercial data centers resulted in annual cost savings of 43%, and migrations from Federal data centers resulted in an average annual cost savings of 12% for similar capabilities.

Recognizing that information technology is constantly improving and changing and that our own IT organization has matured, we are working to increase the integration of previously fragmented Departmental oversight reviews into a defined, efficient governance process that is tailored to the size and criticality of each program. This will result in improved project tracking and oversight and will also help DHS meet our IT-related mission needs.

Security of internal IT systems and networks also remains a priority. DHS continues to enhance the IT security of the Department's internal systems and networks through periodic upgrades to software. In addition, IT staff performs independent validation and verification of implemented corrective actions to address material weaknesses related to financial systems security. All components are implementing a desktop image based on the United States Government Configuration Baseline (USGCB) settings.

Management Integration

Management Integration refers to the development and implementation of consistent and consolidated processes within and across the management functional areas discussed above. From individual performance evaluations to the Department's most costly investment decisions, we have the obligation to operate efficiently and in a manner that best enables us to meet our mission.

The Management Integration area has made substantial progress in the past 3 years, reflected by the fact that both DHS and GAO agree that the majority of the outcomes in the Management Integration area are fully addressed. DHS has made considerable progress towards integrating management across the enterprise. As an example, we have strengthened the delegations of authority to clarify the roles of and enhance oversight between Headquarters and components, and we have implemented the pilot phase of the IILCM to ensure we base investment decisions on closing capability gaps and meeting mission goals and outcomes. Based on the lessons learned from the pilot, the Secretary has determined, through the Unity of Effort initiative, to focus immediate attention on further maturing the Strategy and Capabilities & Requirements phases.

Secretary Johnson and I are committed to integrating all phases of our investment life cycle as we prepare for the fiscal year 2016 budget submission. Advancing the IILCM framework, which is a principal tenet of the Department's overall integration strategy, continues to be a major initiative that builds on the progress we have made. In the near future, as I referenced above, I will oversee a re-constituted Joint Requirements Council as we evaluate fiscal year 2016 resource allocation plans and attempt to harmonize and unify requirements across the DHS enterprise.

The Secretary and I are capitalizing on these previous efforts and broadening them in our "Strengthening Departmental Unity of Effort" initiative. This effort focuses on improving our planning, programming, budgeting, and execution processes through strengthened Departmental structures and increased capability. In making these changes, we will have better traceability between strategic objectives, budgeting, acquisition decisions, operational planning, and mission execution to improve Departmental cohesiveness and operational effectiveness.

We are in the final stages of evolving our business intelligence capability by consolidating management data systems onto a common platform. This effort allows for more current and integrated data across all lines of business, both at headquarters and into DHS's many components.

OTHER DHS HIGH-RISK LIST AREAS

We recognize the critical role that strengthened management functions have in the Department's ability to achieve success. GAO has identified other areas of Department responsibilities that also play an integral role in our mission delivery and, while these non-management areas are not the focus of this hearing, I hope it will be beneficial to this committee for me to provide a brief overview of our work in a few of these areas.

Establishing Effective Mechanisms for Sharing and Managing Terrorism-Related Information to Protect the Homeland

DHS is a key participant in the Federal Information Sharing Environment and continues to develop policies and technical solutions across Sensitive but Unclassified, Secret, and Top Secret/Sensitive Compartmented Information networks that enhance safeguarding and sharing of information with a wide variety of Federal, State, local, and private-sector stakeholders. In January 2013 and immediately following the release of the National Strategy for Information Sharing and Safeguarding, the Department issued the DHS Information Sharing and Safeguarding Strategy focused on goals to share, safeguard, manage, and govern risk, and measure performance. Through a detailed Implementation Plan, the Department has identified key priority objectives with synchronized milestones to effectively execute the Strategy, and has prepared an Implementation Guide that defines the processes to identify gaps, root causes, performance measures, risks, and resourcing for its top information-sharing and safeguarding initiatives.

National Flood Insurance Program

The National Flood Insurance Program (NFIP) serves as the foundation for National efforts to reduce the loss of life and property from flood disasters. NFIP remains on the High-Risk List largely because it does not generate sufficient revenues to repay the billions of dollars borrowed from the U.S. Department of the Treasury to cover claims from the 2005 and 2012 hurricanes or from future catastrophic losses. The lack of sufficient revenues has highlighted structural weaknesses in how the program is funded, including statutorily-mandated subsidies.

DHS and FEMA have been working with GAO to address the challenges identified in GAO's recommendations to improve management and operations. FEMA changed the process for Write Your Own (WYO) company performance under the WYO Financial Control plan, implemented procedures to select statistically representative samples of all claims for conducting claims re-inspections, and requested an independent audit of the NFIP's financial statements. FEMA's focus on implementing GAO recommendations in areas including Strategic Planning, Management and Oversight of the NFIP, and modernizing the NFIP IT system, have resulted in the closure of many of GAO's recommendations. We are actively engaged on those GAO recommendations that remain open.

With the passage of the Biggert-Waters Flood Insurance Act of 2012 and the Homeowners Flood Insurance Affordability Act of 2014, the NFIP now has authority to phase in actuarial rates for some policies and charge policyholders a surcharge, which will improve the financial and operational position of the program over time; however, as a result, policyholders will not pay actuarial rates. Specifically, these two laws raise the statutory limit on annual rate increases, mandate premium increases for certain subsidized policies, establish a reserve fund that will allow the

NFIP to build surplus capital to pay losses in a greater-than-average loss year, and mandate a $25 annual surcharge for most policyholders and a $250 annual surcharge for non-residential properties and residential properties that are not a primary residence, until actuarial rates are reached.

Protecting the Federal Government's Information Systems and the Nation's Cyber Critical Infrastructures

I appreciate GAO's continued engagement on Federal agency cybersecurity and the cybersecurity of critical infrastructure. Since 2009, the Department has managed this area actively, and each subsequent update to the GAO High-Risk List has recognized DHS efforts. The Department works closely with the White House and interagency partners to ensure a whole-of-Government approach to cybersecurity. At the same time, DHS is committed to working with Congress as it explores legislative proposals.

DHS directly supports Federal civilian departments and agencies in developing capabilities that will improve their own cybersecurity posture through the Continuous Diagnostics and Mitigation (CDM) program. One hundred eight departments and agencies are currently covered by Memoranda of Agreement with the CDM program, encompassing over 97 percent of all Federal civilian personnel. In fiscal year 2014, DHS issued the first delivery order for CDM sensors and awarded a contract for the CDM dashboard.

The National Cybersecurity Protection System (NCPS), a key component of which is referred to as EINSTEIN, is an integrated intrusion detection, analytics, information sharing, and intrusion-prevention system designed to support DHS responsibilities for protecting Federal civilian agency networks. These current capabilities, and future capabilities such as CDM, are used by the Department's National Cybersecurity and Communications Integration Center, in concert with its analysis, warning, and incident response capabilities, to protect Federal civilian agencies and assist them when incidents occur. In July 2013, NCPS's EINSTEIN 3 Accelerated (E3A) became operational and provided services to the first Federal agency. With the adoption of E3A, DHS will assume an active role in defending .gov network traffic and significantly reduce the threat vectors available to malicious actors seeking to harm Federal networks. NCPS continues to expand intrusion prevention, information sharing, and cyber analytic capabilities at Federal agencies, marking a critical shift from a passive to an active role in cyber defense and the delivery of enterprise cybersecurity services to decision makers across cybersecurity communities.

With respect to critical infrastructure, the Department continues to grow the critical infrastructure Cyber Information Sharing and Collaboration Program, which is a unique voluntary environment for public-private information sharing and collaboration. In addition, we recently launched the Critical Infrastructure Cyber Community or C3 ("C Cubed") Voluntary Program to assist critical infrastructure owners and operators as they build cybersecurity into their risk management approaches. Much work remains to be completed and we are committed to actively managing this High-Risk area.

When I met with Comptroller General Dodaro, we agreed to develop a set of detailed criteria that GAO and the Department can use to strengthen the Nation's cybersecurity and critical infrastructure resilience. As part of that process, I will receive monthly status updates from DHS components that we will share with GAO.

CONCLUSION

It is our fundamental responsibility to manage the Department of Homeland Security effectively and efficiently. Sound management is critical to our ability to execute our mission successfully, and it is incumbent upon us as guardians of the public trust to be careful and scrupulous in our expenditure of public funds. You have my commitment that I will continue to focus intensely on strengthening the Department's management functions, and that I will work closely with this committee and with GAO to achieve that goal.

Thank you for the opportunity and the privilege to appear before you.

Chairman MCCAUL. Thank you, Deputy Secretary. The Chairman now recognizes Mr. Dodaro for an opening statement.

STATEMENT OF GENE L. DODARO, COMPTROLLER GENERAL OF THE UNITED STATES, GOVERNMENT ACCOUNTABILITY OFFICE

Mr. DODARO. Thank you very much, Mr. Chairman. Good morning to you, Ranking Member Thompson, distinguished Members of the committee. I appreciate the opportunity to be here today to discuss GAO's designations and high-risk areas regarding the Department of Homeland Security.

With regard to the management functions that we initially placed on the list in 2003, I am pleased to report that the Department is well on its way to satisfying two of the five criteria for coming off the list.

One is leadership commitment, and I am very satisfied with the deputy secretary and the Secretary's engagement on this issue. I believe that we have an open, constructive dialogue, which is the first step toward resolving some of these problems.

They also have a pretty good integrated plan for coming off the high-risk list. However, they still need to demonstrate the capacity to make the changes, to have a monitoring effort to make sure that the changes are implemented properly. Most importantly and lastly is they need to demonstrate progress in making sure that they have actually fixed some of the underlying problems that have plagued them in the past.

With regard to the acquisition area, for example, they have designated acquisition components at the component level and organized some centers to bring together some core expertise to help in the acquisitions area. But they need to have governance mechanisms in place to look at the entire acquisition portfolio and set priorities across the Department. Then to make sure that individual acquisitions operate effectively and are more consistently meeting the Department's policies.

For example, 46 percent of the major acquisitions do not have approved baseline cost. About 77 percent do not have yet approved life-cycle cost estimates. So I believe the H.R. 4228 that this committee passed is a very important contribution step forward to putting disciplined acquisition policies in place and having more transparency and accountability for the Department.

With regard to financial management, they have received the clean opinion that both the Chairman and Ranking Member recognized this morning for fiscal year 2013 financial statements. However, to meet our list to get off the list they need to sustain the clean opinion.

They need to get a clean opinion on internal controls, which they are not able to do at this point because of a number of material weaknesses in their systems. They also need to effectively put in modern financial management systems in the components, particularly the Coast Guard, FEMA, ICE, and Customs and Border Patrol.

With regard to human capital management they have put together a plan to guide them in this area. But they must address the root causes that are at the heart of the employee morale issues that have plagued the Department for a number of years. Also to focus on processes to identify skill gaps and to remedy those skill gaps across the Department.

In the IT area we are pleased they have had an enterprise architecture in place, which is a good first step. But they need to finalize their policy governance structure for IT investments, and to expand that policy to cover all 13 portfolios. Right now they have it only covering five of 13. They need to fix their information security weaknesses, which are a major control problem for the Department.

Now with regard to other areas we have on the high-risk list—cybersecurity and critical infrastructure protection that DHS is part of, National Flood Insurance Program, and information sharing in the terrorist information sharing—I would be happy to answer any questions on those areas at the appropriate time.

I would just say with regard to cybersecurity there has been a lot of attention to this area, but more needs to be done. I am very supportive of the H.R. 3696 legislation that you have initiated.

I think the Department has been given responsibility for cybersecurity across the Federal Government without the authority. That authority should be codified and put into law. Also giving them additional guidance in the critical infrastructure protection area and additional codification is a really good step forward.

So I commend this committee both for the acquisition legislation and the cybersecurity and critical infrastructure legislation. So, I would be happy to answer questions at the appropriate point in time. I again very much appreciate the opportunity to be here today to discuss our efforts to help the Department reach its full potential.

[The prepared statement of Mr. Dodaro follows:]

PREPARED STATEMENT OF GENE L. DODARO

MAY 7, 2014

Chairman McCaul, Ranking Member Thompson, and Members of the committee: I am pleased to be here today to discuss our work on the Department of Homeland Security's (DHS) on-going efforts to improve the efficiency of its operations and unity of the Department, with a particular focus on DHS's progress and remaining challenges addressing GAO's high-risk designations. In the 11 years since the Department's creation, DHS has implemented key homeland security operations, achieved important goals and milestones, and grown to more than 240,000 employees and approximately $60 billion in budget authority. During that time, our work has identified several areas where DHS needs to address gaps and weaknesses in its current operational and implementation efforts, as well as strengthen the efficiency and effectiveness of those efforts. Since 2003, we have made approximately 2,100 recommendations to DHS to strengthen program management, performance measurement efforts, and management processes, among other things. DHS has implemented more than 65 percent of these recommendations and has actions under way to address others.

We also report regularly to the Congress on Government operations that we identified as high-risk because of their greater vulnerability to fraud, waste, abuse, and mismanagement, or the need for transformation to address economy, efficiency, or effectiveness challenges. DHS has sole or critical responsibility for four GAO high-risk areas—(1) *Strengthening DHS Management Functions*, (2) *National Flood Insurance Program (NFIP)*, (3) *Protecting the Federal Government's Information Systems and the Nation's Cyber Critical Infrastructures*, and (4) *Establishing Effective Mechanisms for Sharing and Managing Terrorism-Related Information to Protect the Homeland*. DHS has made progress addressing areas we have identified as high-risk, but needs to continue to strengthen its efforts in order to more efficiently and effectively achieve its homeland security missions. In particular:

- In 2003, we designated implementing and transforming DHS as high-risk because DHS had to transform 22 agencies—several with major management challenges—into one department, and failure to address associated risks could have serious consequences for U.S. National and economic security.[1] While challenges remain across its missions, DHS has made considerable progress in transforming its original component agencies into a single department. As a result, in our 2013 high-risk update, we narrowed the scope of the high-risk area to focus on strengthening DHS management functions (human capital, acquisition, financial management, and information technology [IT]).[2]

- In 2006, we added the NFIP—a key component of the Federal Government's efforts to limit the damage and financial impact of floods—to the GAO high-risk list because the program faced significant on-going financial and management challenges.[3] In particular, the NFIP, which is managed by DHS's Federal Emergency Management Agency (FEMA), is unlikely to generate sufficient revenue to cover future catastrophic losses or repay billions of dollars borrowed from the Department of the Treasury to cover insurance claims from previous disasters.

- In 1997, we designated Federal information security as a Government-wide high-risk area, and we expanded the area in 2003 to include systems supporting critical infrastructure such as power distribution, communications, banking and finance, water supply, National defense, and emergency services.[4] The effective security of these systems and the data they contain is essential to National security, economic well-being, and public health and safety. DHS is responsible for securing its own information systems and data and also plays a pivotal role in Government-wide cybersecurity efforts.

- In 2005, we designated the sharing of terrorism-related information as high-risk because of the significant challenges the Federal Government faces in sharing this information in a timely, accurate, and useful manner.[5] The sharing of terrorism-related information is a Government-wide effort that involves numerous Federal departments and agencies. DHS plays a critical role in this sharing given its homeland security missions and responsibilities.

In November 2000, we published our criteria for removing areas from the high-risk list.[6] Specifically, agencies must have (1) a demonstrated strong commitment and top leadership support to address the risks; (2) a corrective action plan that identifies the root causes, identifies effective solutions, and provides for substantially completing corrective measures in the near term, including but not limited to steps necessary to implement solutions we recommended; (3) the capacity (that is, the people and other resources) to resolve the risks; (4) a program instituted to monitor and independently validate the effectiveness and sustainability of corrective measures; and (5) the ability to demonstrate progress in implementing corrective measures. When legislative, administration, and agency actions, including those in response to our recommendations, result in significant progress toward resolving a high-risk problem, we remove the high-risk area.

My testimony today discusses our observations on DHS's progress and work remaining in addressing: (1) High-risk areas for which DHS has sole responsibility, and (2) high-risk areas for which DHS has critical, but shared, responsibility.

This statement is based on GAO's 2013 high-risk update as well as reports and testimonies we issued from March 2013 through April 2014.[7] For the past products, among other things, we analyzed DHS strategies and other documents related to the Department's efforts to address its high-risk areas; reviewed our past reports issued since DHS began its operations in March 2003; and interviewed DHS officials. More detailed information on the scope and methodology of our prior work can be found within each specific report. This statement is also based on analyses from our ongoing assessment of DHS's efforts to address its high-risk areas since February 2013. We expect to report final results from this work in our 2015 high-risk update. For our analyses, among other things, we analyzed DHS documentation, such as Departmental guidance, and met with DHS officials, including the deputy secretary and under secretary for management, to discuss DHS's efforts to address its high-risk areas. With respect to the *Strengthening DHS Management Functions* high-risk area, on May 1, 2014, DHS provided us with an updated version of its *Integrated*

[1] GAO, *High-Risk Series: An Update*, GAO–03–119 (Washington, DC: January 2003).

[2] GAO, *High-Risk Series: An Update*, GAO–13–283 (Washington, DC: February 2013). For additional information, see our high-risk list key issues page at *http://www.gao.gov/highrisk/overview*.

[3] GAO, *GAO's High-Risk Program*, GAO–06–497T (Washington, DC: Mar. 15, 2006).

[4] GAO–03–119.

[5] GAO, *High-Risk Series: An Update*, GAO–05–207 (Washington, DC: Jan. 1, 2005).

[6] GAO, *Determining Performance and Accountability Challenges and High Risks*, GAO–01–159SP (Washington, DC: Nov. 1, 2000).

[7] GAO–13–283.

Strategy for High-Risk Management. We plan to analyze this update as part of our on-going assessment of DHS's progress in addressing this high-risk area.

We conducted the work on which this statement is based in accordance with generally accepted Government auditing standards. Those standards require that we plan and perform the audit to obtain sufficient, appropriate evidence to provide a reasonable basis for our findings and conclusions based on our audit objectives. We believe that the evidence obtained provides a reasonable basis for our findings and conclusions based on our audit objectives.

HIGH-RISK AREAS FOR WHICH DHS HAS SOLE RESPONSIBILITY

DHS has made progress in addressing high-risk areas for which it has sole responsibility, but significant work remains.

Strengthening DHS Management Functions

DHS has made important progress in implementing, transforming, strengthening, and integrating its management functions in human capital, acquisition, financial management, and IT. This has included taking numerous actions specifically designed to address our criteria for removing areas from the high-risk list. However, as we reported in our February 2013 high-risk update, this area remains high-risk because the Department has significant work ahead.[8] As shown in Table 1, DHS has met two of our criteria for removal from the high-risk list (leadership commitment and a corrective action plan), and has partially met the remaining three criteria (a framework to monitor progress; capacity; and demonstrated, sustained progress).

TABLE 1.—ASSESSMENT OF DEPARTMENT OF HOMELAND SECURITY (DHS) PROGRESS IN ADDRESSING THE STRENGTHENING DHS MANAGEMENT FUNCTIONS HIGH-RISK AREA, AS OF MAY 2014

Criterion for Removal From the High-Risk List	Met [1]	Partially Met [2]	Not Met [3]
Leadership commitment	X		
Corrective action plan	X		
Capacity		X	
Framework to monitor progress		X	
Demonstrated, sustained progress		X	
Total	2	3	0

Source: GAO analysis of DHS documents, interviews, and prior GAO reports.

[1] "Met": There are no significant actions that need to be taken to further address this criterion.

[2] "Partially met": Some but not all actions necessary to generally meet the criterion have been taken.

[3] "Not met": Few, if any, actions toward meeting the criterion have been taken.

Leadership commitment (met).—The Secretary and deputy secretary of Homeland Security, the under secretary for management at DHS, and other senior officials have continued to demonstrate commitment and top leadership support for addressing the Department's management challenges. They have also taken actions to institutionalize this commitment to help ensure the long-term success of the Department's efforts. For example, in May 2012, the Secretary of Homeland Security modified the delegations of authority between the Management Directorate and its counterparts at the component level to clarify and strengthen the authorities of the under secretary for management across the Department.

In addition, in April 2014, the Secretary of Homeland Security issued a memorandum committing to improving DHS's planning, programming, budgeting, and execution processes through strengthened Departmental structures and increased capability. This memorandum identified several initial areas of focus intended to build organizational capacity.[9] Senior DHS officials have also routinely met with us over the past 5 years to discuss the Department's plans and progress in addressing this high-risk area, during which we provided specific feedback on the Department's efforts. According to these officials, and as demonstrated through their progress, the Department is committed to demonstrating measurable, sustained progress in ad-

[8] GAO–13–283.

[9] DHS, Secretary of Homeland Security, *Strengthening Departmental Unity of Effort*, Memorandum for DHS Leadership (Washington, DC: April 22, 2014).

dressing this high-risk area. It will be important for DHS to maintain its current level of top leadership support and sustained commitment to ensure continued progress in successfully executing its corrective actions through completion.

Corrective action plan (met).—DHS established a plan for addressing this high-risk area. In a September 2010 letter to DHS, we identified and DHS agreed to achieve 31 actions and outcomes that are critical to addressing the challenges within the Department's management areas and in integrating those functions across the Department. In January 2011, DHS issued its initial *Integrated Strategy for High-Risk Management,* which included key management initiatives and related corrective action plans for addressing its management challenges and the outcomes we identified. DHS provided updates of its progress in implementing these initiatives and corrective actions in its later versions of the strategy. In March 2014, we made updates to the actions and outcomes in collaboration with DHS to reduce overlap and ensure their continued relevance and appropriateness. These updates resulted in a reduction from 31 to 30 total actions and outcomes.

DHS's strategy and approach to continuously refining actionable steps to implementing the outcomes, if implemented effectively and sustained, provide a path for DHS to be removed from GAO's high-risk list.

Capacity (partially met).—In May 2014, DHS identified that it had resources needed to implement 7 of the 11 initiatives the Department had under way to address the actions and outcomes, but did not identify sufficient resource needs for the 4 remaining initiatives. In our analysis of DHS's June 2013 update, which similarly did not identify sufficient resource needs for all initiatives, we found that this absence of complete resource information made it difficult to fully assess the extent to which DHS has the capacity to implement its initiatives.

In addition, our prior work has identified specific capacity gaps that could undermine achievement of management outcomes. For example, in September 2012, we reported that 51 of 62 acquisition programs faced workforce shortfalls in program management, cost estimating, engineering, and other areas, increasing the likelihood that the programs will perform poorly in the future.[10] Since that time, DHS has appointed component acquisition executives at the components and made progress in filling staff positions. In April 2014, however, we reported that DHS needed to increase its cost-estimating capacity, and that the Department had not approved baselines for 21 of 46 major acquisition programs.[11] These baselines—which establish cost, schedule, and capability parameters—are necessary to accurately assess program performance.

DHS needs to continue to identify resources for the remaining initiatives; determine that sufficient resources and staff are committed to initiatives; work to mitigate shortfalls and prioritize initiatives, as needed; and communicate to senior leadership critical resource gaps.

Framework to monitor progress (partially met).—DHS established a framework for monitoring its progress in implementing the corrective actions it identified for addressing the 30 actions and outcomes. In the June 2012 update to the *Integrated Strategy for High-Risk Management,* DHS included, for the first time, performance measures to track its progress in implementing all of its key management initiatives. DHS continued to include performance measures in its May 2014 update.

Additionally, in March 2014, the deputy secretary began meeting monthly with the DHS management team to discuss DHS's progress in strengthening its management functions. According to senior DHS officials, as part of these meetings, attendees discuss a report that senior DHS officials update each month, which identifies corrective actions for each outcome, as well as projected and actual completion dates.

However, there are opportunities for DHS to strengthen this framework. For example, as we reported in September 2013, DHS components need to develop performance and functionality targets for assessing their proposed financial systems.[12] This would include having an independent validation and verification program in place to ensure the modernized financial systems meet expected targets. Moving forward, DHS will need to closely track and independently validate the effectiveness

---

[10] GAO, *Homeland Security: DHS Requires More Disciplined Investment Management to Help Meet Mission Needs,* GAO–12–833 (Washington, DC: Sept. 18, 2012).

[11] GAO, *Homeland Security Acquisitions: DHS Could Better Manage Its Portfolio to Address Funding Gaps and Improve Communications with Congress,* GAO–14–332 (Washington, DC: Apr. 17, 2014).

[12] GAO, *DHS Financial Management: Additional Efforts Needed to Resolve Deficiencies in Internal Controls and Financial Management Systems,* GAO–13–561 (Washington, DC: Sept. 30, 2013).

and sustainability of its corrective actions and make mid-course adjustments, as needed.

Demonstrated, sustained progress (partially met).—Key to addressing the Department's management challenges is DHS demonstrating the ability to achieve sustained progress across the 30 actions and outcomes we identified and DHS agreed were needed to address the high-risk area. These actions and outcomes include, among others, validating required acquisition documents in accordance with a Department-approved, knowledge-based acquisition process, and sustaining clean audit opinions for at least 2 consecutive years on Department-wide financial statements and internal controls. As illustrated by the examples below, DHS has made important progress in implementing corrective actions across its management functions, but it has not demonstrated sustainable, measurable progress in addressing key challenges that remain within these functions and in the integration of those functions.[13]

Human capital management.—DHS has mostly addressed 1 of the 7 human capital management outcomes and partially addressed the remaining 6. For example, as we reported in December 2012, DHS has developed and demonstrated progress in implementing a strategic human capital plan.[14] This plan, among other things, is integrated with broader organizational strategic planning, and mostly addresses this outcome. However, DHS needs to improve other aspects of its human capital management.

- As we reported in December 2013, the Office of Personnel Management's 2013 Federal Employee Viewpoint Survey data showed that DHS employee satisfaction was 36th of 37 Federal agencies and had decreased 7 percentage points since 2011, which is more than the Government-wide decrease of 4 percentage points over the same time period.[15] As a result, the gap between average DHS employee satisfaction and the Government-wide average widened to 7 percentage points.[16] Accordingly, DHS has considerable work ahead to improve its employee morale.
- Further, according to senior DHS officials, the Department has efforts under way intended to link workforce planning efforts to strategic and program-specific planning efforts to identify current and future human capital needs, including the knowledge, skills, and abilities needed for the Department to meet its goals and objectives. According to these officials, the Department is in the process of finalizing competency gap assessments to identify potential skills gaps within its components that collectively encompass almost half of the Department's workforce. These assessments focus on occupations DHS identifies as critical to its mission, including emergency management specialists and cyber-focused IT management personnel. DHS plans to analyze the results of these assessments and develop plans to address any gaps the assessments identify by the end of fiscal year 2014. This is a positive step, as identifying skills gaps could help the Department to better identify current and future human capital needs and ensure the Department possesses the knowledge, skills, and abilities needed to meet its goals and objectives. Given that DHS is finalizing these assessments, it is too early to assess their effectiveness.

Acquisition management.—DHS has mostly addressed one of the five acquisition management outcomes, partially addressed one, and initiated activities to address the remaining three. DHS has made the most progress in increasing component-level acquisition capability by, for example, establishing a component acquisition executive in each DHS component to provide oversight and support programs within its portfolio. DHS has also taken steps to enhance its acquisition workforce by establishing centers of excellence for cost estimating, systems engineering, and other disciplines to promote best practices and provide technical guidance. However, DHS needs to improve its acquisition management. For example:

- DHS initiated a governance body in 2013 to review and validate acquisition programs' requirements and identify and eliminate any unintended redundancies, but it considered trade-offs only across acquisition programs within the Depart-

---

[13] For our assessments of DHS's progress in addressing the 30 outcomes, "fully addressed" means the outcome is fully addressed; "mostly addressed" means progress is significant and a small amount of work remains; "partially addressed" means progress is measurable, but significant work remains; and "initiated" means activities have been initiated to address outcomes, but it is too early to report progress.

[14] GAO, *DHS Strategic Workforce Planning: Oversight of Department-wide Efforts Should Be Strengthened*, GAO–13–65 (Washington, DC: Dec. 3, 2012). For example:

[15] The Federal Employee Viewpoint Survey measures employees' perceptions of whether and to what extent conditions characterizing successful organizations are present in their agencies.

[16] GAO, *Department of Homeland Security: DHS's Efforts to Improve Employee Morale and Fill Senior Leadership Vacancies*, GAO–14–228T (Washington, DC: Dec. 12, 2013).

ment's cybersecurity portfolio. DHS acknowledged that the Department has no formal structure in place to consider trade-offs DHS-wide, but DHS anticipates chartering such a body by the end of May 2014.

- DHS also has initiated efforts to validate required acquisition documents in accordance with a knowledge-based acquisition process, but this remains a major challenge for the Department. A knowledge-based approach provides developers with information needed to make sound investment decisions, and it would help DHS address significant challenges we have identified across its acquisition programs.[17] DHS's acquisition policy largely reflects key acquisition management practices, but the Department has not implemented it consistently. In March 2014, we reported that the Transportation Security Administration does not collect or analyze available information that could be used to enhance the effectiveness of its advanced imaging technology.[18] In March 2014, we also found that U.S. Customs and Border Protection (CBP) did not fully follow DHS policy regarding testing for the integrated fixed towers being deployed on the Arizona border.[19] As a result, DHS does not have complete information on how the towers will operate once they are fully deployed.
- Finally, DHS does not have the acquisition management tools in place to consistently demonstrate whether its major acquisition programs are on track to achieve their cost, schedule, and capability goals. About half of major programs lack an approved baseline, and 77 percent lack approved life-cycle cost estimates. DHS stated in its 2014 update that it will take time to demonstrate substantive progress in this area. We have recently initiated two reviews to examine DHS's progress in these high-risk areas. In addition, the House Homeland Security committee recently introduced a DHS acquisition reform bill that reinforces the importance of key acquisition management practices, such as establishing cost, schedule, and capability parameters, and includes requirements to better identify and address poor-performing acquisition programs, which could aid the Department in addressing its acquisition management challenges.

Financial management.—DHS has made progress toward improving its financial management and has fully addressed 1 of 8 high-risk financial management outcomes—ensuring its financial statements are accurate and reliable.[20] However, a significant amount of work remains to be completed on the other 7 outcomes related to DHS's financial statements, internal control over financial reporting, and modernizing financial management systems.

- DHS produced accurate and reliable financial statements for the first time in fiscal year 2013, in part through management's commitment to improving its financial management process. As of May 2014, DHS is working toward sustaining this key achievement.
- DHS has also made some progress toward implementing effective internal control over financial reporting, in part by implementing a corrective action planning process aimed at addressing internal control weaknesses. For example, the Department took corrective actions to reduce the material weakness in environmental and other liabilities to a significant deficiency.[21] However, DHS needs to eliminate all material weaknesses at the Department level before its financial auditor can assert that the controls are effective. For example, one of the material weaknesses involves deficiencies in property, plant, and equipment. DHS plans to achieve this outcome for fiscal year 2016. To meet another outcome, DHS needs to sustain these efforts for 2 years.
- DHS also needs to effectively manage the modernization of financial management systems at the U.S. Coast Guard (USCG), U.S. Immigration and Customs

---

[17] In our past work examining weapon acquisition issues and best practices for product development, we have found that leading commercial firms pursue an acquisition approach that is anchored in knowledge, whereby high levels of product knowledge are demonstrated by critical points in the acquisition process.

[18] GAO, *Advanced Imaging Technology: TSA Needs Additional Information Before Procuring Next-Generation Systems,* GAO–14–357 (Washington, DC: March 31, 2014).

[19] GAO, *Arizona Border Surveillance Technology Plan: Additional Actions Needed to Strengthen Management and Assess Effectiveness,* GAO–14–368 (Washington, DC: Mar. 3, 2014).

[20] The financial management outcomes have twice been revised since September 2010 when they were initially established. The most recent revision occurred in March 2014 when GAO and DHS agreed to revise the outcomes to clarify certain requirements and eliminate overlap among the outcomes and between the outcomes and GAO's high-risk removal criteria.

[21] Environmental liabilities consist of environmental remediation, clean-up, and decommissioning. A significant deficiency is a deficiency, or combination of deficiencies, in internal control important enough to merit attention by those charged with governance. A material weakness is a significant deficiency, or a combination of significant deficiencies, in internal control such that there is a reasonable possibility that a material misstatement of the entity's financial statements will not be prevented, or detected and corrected, on a timely basis.

Enforcement (ICE), and the Federal Emergency Management Agency (FEMA). Both USCG and ICE have made some progress toward modernizing their systems and foresee moving to a Federal shared service provider and completing their efforts in the latter part of 2016 and 2017.[22] Because of critical stability issues with its legacy financial system that were resolved in May 2013, FEMA postponed its modernization efforts and has not restarted them.

IT Management.—DHS has fully addressed 1 of the 6 IT management outcomes and partially addressed the remaining 5. In particular, the Department has strengthened its enterprise architecture program (or blueprint) to guide IT acquisitions by, among other things, largely addressing our prior recommendations aimed at adding needed architectural depth and breadth, thus fully addressing this outcome. However, the Department needs to continue to demonstrate progress in strengthening other core IT management areas. For example,

- While the Department is taking the necessary steps to enhance its IT security program, such as finalizing its annual Information Security Performance Plan, further work will be needed for DHS to eliminate the Department's current material weakness in its information security. It will be important for the Department to fully implement its plan, since DHS's financial statement auditor reported in December 2013 that flaws in the security controls such as access controls, contingency planning, and segregation of duties were a material weakness for financial reporting purposes.
- While important steps have been taken to define IT investment management processes generally consistent with best practices, work is needed to demonstrate progress in implementing these processes across DHS's 13 IT investment portfolios.[23] In July 2012, we recommended that DHS finalize the policies and procedures associated with its new tiered IT governance structure and continue to implement key processes supporting this structure.[24] DHS agreed with these recommendations; however, as of April 2014, the Department had not finalized the key IT governance directive, and the draft structure has been implemented across only 5 of the 13 investment portfolios. [25]

Fully addressing these actions would also help DHS to address key IT operations efficiency initiatives, as well as to more systematically identify other opportunities for savings. For example, as part of the Office of Management and Budget's data center consolidation initiative, we reported that DHS planned to consolidate from 101 data centers to 37 data centers by December 2015.[26] Further, DHS officials told us that the Department had achieved actual cost savings totaling about $140 million in fiscal years 2011 through 2013, and that it estimates total consolidation cost savings of approximately $650 million through fiscal year 2019.

- DHS has also made progress in establishing and implementing sound IT system acquisition processes, but continued efforts are needed to ensure that the Department's major IT acquisition programs are applying these processes and obtaining more predictable outcomes. In 2013, DHS's Office of the Chief Information Officer led an assessment of its major IT programs (against industry best practices in key IT system acquisition process areas) to determine its capability strengths and weaknesses, and has work under way to track programs' progress in addressing identified capability gaps, such as requirements management and risk analysis. While this gap analysis and approach for tracking implementation of corrective actions are important steps, DHS will need to show that these actions are resulting in better, more predictable outcomes for its major IT system acquisitions. Demonstrated progress in closing these gaps is especially important in light of our recent reports on major DHS IT programs experiencing significant challenges largely because of system acquisition process shortfalls, in-

---

[22] A shared service provider is a third-party entity that manages and distributes software-based services and solutions to customers across a wide area network from a central data center.

[23] The 13 portfolios are intelligence, domain awareness, securing, screening, law enforcement, information sharing and safeguarding, continuity-of-operations planning, benefits administration, incident management, enterprise business services, enterprise financial management, enterprise IT services, and enterprise human capital.

[24] GAO, *Information Technology: DHS Needs to Further Define and Implement Its New Governance Process,* GAO–12–818 (Washington, DC: July 25, 2012).

[25] The draft structure has been implemented across the following five portfolios: Intelligence, screening, information sharing and safeguarding, enterprise IT services, and enterprise human capital.

[26] GAO, *Data Center Consolidation: Agencies Making Progress on Efforts, but Inventories and Plans Need to Be Completed,* GAO–12–742 (Washington, DC: July 19, 2012).

cluding DHS's major border security system modernization, known as TECS-Mod.[27]

Management integration.—DHS has made substantial progress integrating its management functions, fully addressing 3 of the 4 outcomes we identified as key to the Department's management integration efforts. For example, DHS issued a comprehensive plan to guide its management integration efforts—the *Integrated Strategy for High-Risk Management*—in January 2011, and has generally improved upon this plan with each update. In addition, in April 2014, the Secretary of Homeland Security issued a memorandum committing to improving DHS's planning, programming, budgeting, and execution processes through strengthened Departmental structures and increased capability.[28] To achieve the last and most significant outcome—implement actions and outcomes in each management area to develop consistent or consolidated processes and systems within and across its management functional areas—DHS needs to continue to demonstrate sustainable progress integrating its management functions within and across the Department and its components and take additional actions to further and more effectively integrate the Department.

For example, recognizing the need to better integrate its lines of business, in February 2013, the Secretary of Homeland Security signed a policy directive establishing the principles of the Integrated Investment Life-Cycle Management to guide planning, executing, and managing critical investments Department-wide. DHS's June 2013 *Integrated Strategy for High-Risk Management* identified that Integrated Investment Life-Cycle Management will require significant changes to DHS planning, executing, and managing critical investments. At that time, DHS was piloting elements of the framework to inform a portion of the fiscal year 2015 budget. DHS's May 2014 strategy update states that the Department plans to receive an independent analysis of the pilots in May 2014. Given that these efforts are under way, it is too early to assess their impact.

As we reported in March 2013, to more fully address the *Strengthening DHS Management Functions* high-risk area, DHS needs to continue implementing its *Integrated Strategy for High-Risk Management* and show measurable, sustainable progress in implementing its key management initiatives and corrective actions and achieving outcomes.[29] In doing so, it will be important for DHS to:

- maintain its current level of top leadership support and sustained commitment to ensure continued progress in executing its corrective actions through completion;
- continue to implement its plan for addressing this high-risk area and periodically report its progress to Congress and GAO;
- monitor the effectiveness of its efforts to establish reliable resource estimates at the Department and component levels, address and work to mitigate any resource gaps, and prioritize initiatives as needed to ensure it has the capacity to implement and sustain its corrective actions;
- closely track and independently validate the effectiveness and sustainability of its corrective actions and make midcourse adjustments, as needed; and
- make continued progress in addressing the 30 actions and outcomes—for the majority of which significant work remains—and demonstrate that systems, personnel, and policies are in place to ensure that progress can be sustained over time.[30]

We will continue to monitor DHS's efforts in this high-risk area to determine if the actions and outcomes are achieved and sustained.

National Flood Insurance Program

FEMA has made progress in all of the areas required for removal of the NFIP from the high-risk list, but needs to initiate or complete additional actions; also, recent legislation has created challenges for FEMA in addressing the financial exposure created by the program. FEMA leadership has displayed a commitment to addressing these challenges and has made progress in a number of areas, such as financial reporting and continuity planning. While FEMA has plans for addressing and tracking progress on our specific recommendations, it has yet to address many of them. For example, FEMA has not completed actions in certain areas, such as modernizing its claims and policy management system and overseeing compensation

---

[27] GAO, *Border Security: DHS's Efforts to Modernize Key Enforcement Systems Could be Strengthened*, GAO–14–62 (Washington, DC: Dec. 5, 2013).

[28] DHS, *Secretary of Homeland Security, Strengthening Departmental Unity of Effort*, Memorandum for DHS Leadership (Washington, DC: April 22, 2014).

[29] GAO, *High-Risk Series, Government-wide 2013 Update and Progress Made by the Department of Homeland Security*, GAO–13–444T (Washington, DC: March 21, 2013).

[30] GAO–13–444T.

of insurers that sell NFIP policies. Completing such actions will likely help improve the financial stability and operations of the program. Table 2 summarizes DHS's progress in addressing the NFIP high-risk area.

TABLE 2.—ASSESSMENT OF DEPARTMENT OF HOMELAND SECURITY PROGRESS IN ADDRESSING THE NATIONAL FLOOD INSURANCE PROGRAM HIGH-RISK AREA, AS OF MAY 2014

Criterion for Removal From the High-Risk List	Met [1]	Partially Met [2]	Not Met [3]
Leadership commitment		X	
Corrective action plan		X	
Capacity		X	
Framework to monitor progress		X	
Demonstrated, sustained progress		X	
Total	0	5	0

Source: GAO analysis of Federal Emergency Management Agency documents, interviews, and prior GAO reports.

[1] "Met": There are no significant actions that need to be taken to further address this criterion.

[2] "Partially met": Some but not all actions necessary to generally meet the criterion have been taken.

[3] "Not met": Few, if any, actions toward meeting the criterion have been taken.

Leadership commitment (partially met). FEMA officials responsible for the NFIP have shown a commitment to taking a number of actions to implement our recommendations, which are designed to improve both the financial stability and operations of the program. For example, they have indicated a commitment to implementing our recommendations and have been proactive in clarifying and taking the actions needed to do so. In addition, FEMA officials have met with us to discuss outstanding recommendations, the actions they have taken to address them, and additional actions they could take. Further, a DHS official said that FEMA holds regular meetings to discuss the status of open recommendations.

Recent legislative changes, however, have presented challenges for FEMA in addressing the financial exposure created by the NFIP. For example, in July 2012, the Biggert-Waters Flood Insurance Reform Act of 2012 (Biggert-Waters Act) was enacted, containing provisions to help strengthen the future financial solvency and administrative efficiency of NFIP, including phasing out almost all discounted insurance premiums (commonly referred to as subsidized premiums).[31] In July 2013, we reported that FEMA was starting to implement some of the required changes.[32] However, on March 21, 2014, the Homeowner Flood Insurance Affordability Act of 2014 (2014 Act) was enacted, reinstating certain premium subsidies and restoring grandfathered rates removed by the Biggert-Waters Act.[33] The 2014 Act addresses affordability concerns for certain property owners, but may also increase NFIP's long-term financial burden on taxpayers.[34]

Corrective action plan (partially met).—While FEMA developed corrective action plans for implementing the recommendations in individual GAO reports, it has not developed a comprehensive plan to address the issues that have placed the NFIP on GAO's high-risk list. While addressing our recommendations is part of such a plan, a comprehensive plan also defines the root causes, identifies effective solutions, and provides for substantially completing corrective measures near term. According to a DHS official, the individual action plans collectively represent their plan for addressing these issues, as the recommendations cover steps needed to improve the program's financial stability as well as its administration. The official added that DHS has developed more comprehensive plans for other high-risk areas, which have been helpful, and could consider doing so for the NFIP, but such plans require a lot of work. Such a plan could help FEMA ensure that all important issues, and all aspects of those issues, are addressed. For example, while our recommendations regarding the NFIP's financial stability have focused on the extent

[31] Pub. L. No. 112–141, Div. F, Title II, Subtit. A, 126 Stat. 405, 916 (July 6, 2012).

[32] GAO, *Flood Insurance: More Information Needed on Subsidized Properties,* GAO–13–607 (Washington, DC: July 3, 2013).

[33] Pub. L. No. 113–89, 128 Stat. 1020 (Mar. 21, 2014).

[34] GAO, *Flood Insurance: Strategies for Increasing Private Sector Involvement,* GAO–14–127 (Washington, DC: Jan. 22, 2014).

of subsidized rates and the rate-setting process, financial stability could include other important areas, such as debt management. As of December 2013, FEMA owed the Treasury $24 billion—primarily to pay claims associated with Superstorm Sandy (2012) and Hurricane Katrina (2005)—and had not made a principal payment since 2010.

Capacity (partially met).—FEMA faces several challenges in improving the program's financial stability and operations. First, recent legislative changes permit certain premium subsidies and restore grandfathered rates removed by the Biggert-Waters Act. These provisions, along with others, may weaken the potential for improved financial soundness of the NFIP program. Second, while FEMA is establishing a reserve fund as required by the Biggert-Waters Act, it is unlikely to initially meet the act's annual targets for building up the reserve, partly because of statutory limitations on annual premium increases. Third, while FEMA has begun taking some actions to improve its administration of the NFIP, it is unclear how the resources required to implement both the Biggert-Waters Act and the 2014 Act will affect its ability to continue and complete these efforts. For example, the Acts require FEMA to complete multiple studies and take a number of actions within the next several years, which will require resources FEMA would normally have committed to other efforts.

Monitoring Progress (partially met).—FEMA has a process in place to monitor progress in taking actions to implement our recommendations related to the NFIP. For example, the status of efforts to address the recommendations is regularly discussed both within the Flood Insurance and Mitigation Administration, which administers the NFIP, and at the DHS level, according to a DHS official. However, it does not have a specific process for independently validating the effectiveness or sustainability of those actions. Instead, according to a DHS official, once a recommendation related to the NFIP is implemented, the effects of the actions taken to do so are not tracked separately, but are evaluated as part of regular reviews of the effectiveness of the entire program. Broader monitoring of the effectiveness and sustainability of its actions would help ensure that appropriate corrective actions are being taken.

Demonstrated, sustained progress (partially met).—FEMA has begun to take actions to improve the program's financial stability, such as initiating actions to improve the accuracy of full-risk rates.[35] However, these efforts are not complete, and FEMA does not have some information, such as the number and location of existing grandfathered properties and information necessary to appropriately revise premium rates for previously subsidized properties.[36] Similarly, FEMA has taken a number of actions to improve areas of the program's operations, such as financial reporting and continuity planning.[37] However, some important actions, such as modernizing its policy and claims management system and ensuring the reasonableness of compensation to insurance companies that sell and service most NFIP policies, remain to be completed.[38] Sustained progress will be needed for FEMA to address the financial and operational issues facing NFIP.

GOVERNMENT-WIDE HIGH-RISK AREAS IN WHICH DHS PLAYS A CRITICAL ROLE

Progress has been made in the Government-wide high-risk areas in which DHS plays a critical role, but significant work remains.

Information Security and Cyber Critical Infrastructure Protection

As we reported in our February 2013 high-risk update, the White House and Federal agencies, including DHS, have taken a variety of actions that were intended to enhance Federal and critical infrastructure cybersecurity. For example, the Government issued numerous strategy-related documents over the past decade and established agency performance goals and a mechanism to monitor performance in three cross-agency priority areas of strong authentication, Trusted Internet Connections, and continuous monitoring.[39]

---

[35] GAO, *Flood Insurance: FEMA's Rate-Setting Process Warrants Attention,* GAO–09–12 (Washington, DC: Oct. 31, 2008).

[36] GAO–13–607.

[37] GAO, *FEMA: Action Needed to Improve Administration of the National Flood Insurance Program,* GAO–11–297 (Washington, DC: June 9, 2011).

[38] GAO, *Flood Insurance: Opportunities Exist to Improve Oversight of the WYO Program,* GAO–09–455 (Washington, DC: Aug. 21, 2009) and GAO–11–297.

[39] Strong authentication involves increasing the use of Federal smartcard credentials such as Personal Identity Verification and Common Access Cards that provide multi-factor authentication and digital signature and encryption capabilities, authorizing users to access Federal infor-

Continued

In addition, since the February 2013 high-risk update, the administration has continued its cyber-related efforts. In February 2013, the President issued Presidential Policy Directive 21 on critical infrastructure security and resilience [40] and Executive Order 13636 on improving critical infrastructure cybersecurity. [41] These documents assign specific actions to particular individuals and agencies with specific time frames for completion.

However, more efforts are needed by Federal organizations, including the White House, DHS, and other agencies, to address a number of areas. To illustrate the scope and persistence of this challenge, in fiscal year 2013, inspectors general at 21 of the 24 agencies cited information security as a major management challenge for their agencies, [42] and 18 agencies reported that information security control deficiencies were either a material weakness or a significant deficiency in internal controls over financial reporting in fiscal year 2013. [43]

DHS's Role in Federal Information Security and Cyber Critical Infrastructure Protection

In addition to having responsibilities for securing its own information systems and data, DHS plays a pivotal role in Government-wide cybersecurity efforts. In particular, in July 2010, the Director of the Office of Management and Budget (OMB) and the White House Cybersecurity Coordinator issued a joint memorandum that transferred several key OMB responsibilities under the Federal Information Security Management Act of 2002 (FISMA) to DHS. [44] Specifically, DHS is to exercise primary responsibility within the Executive branch for overseeing and assisting with the operational aspects of cybersecurity for Federal systems that fall within the scope of FISMA.

We agree that DHS should play a role in the operational aspects of Federal cybersecurity. We suggested in February 2013 that Congress consider legislation that would clarify roles and responsibilities for implementing and overseeing Federal information security programs and for protecting the Nation's critical cyber assets. [45]

Regarding cyber critical infrastructure protection, a fundamental component of DHS's efforts is its partnership approach, whereby it engages in partnerships among Government and industry stakeholders. Such an approach is essential because the majority of critical infrastructure in the United States is owned and operated by the private sector. In 2006, DHS issued the National Infrastructure Protection Plan. The plan, subsequently updated several times, provides the overarching approach for integrating the Nation's critical infrastructure protection and resilience activities into a single National effort. [46] Congress is considering several bills that would address cyber information sharing and the cybersecurity posture of the Federal Government and the Nation. For example, H.R. 3696, the National Cybersecurity and Critical Infrastructure Protection Act of 2014, would address DHS's role and responsibilities in protecting Federal civilian information systems and critical infrastructure from cyber threats. [47]

Specific laws, Executive Orders, and directives have further guided DHS's role in cyber critical infrastructure protection. For example, Executive Order 13636 directs

---

mation systems with a higher level of assurance. Trusted Internet Connections is an initiative to consolidate external telecommunication connections and ensure a set of baseline security capabilities for situational awareness and enhanced monitoring. Continuous monitoring of Federal information systems includes transforming the otherwise static security control assessment and authorization process into a dynamic risk mitigation program that provides essential, near-real-time security status and remediation, increasing visibility into system operations and helping security personnel make risk management decisions based on increased situational awareness.

[40] The White House, Presidential Policy Directive/PPD–21, Critical Infrastructure Security and Resilience (Feb. 12, 2013).

[41] Exec. Order No. 13,636, 78 Fed. Reg. 11,739 (Feb. 19, 2013).

[42] The 24 major departments and agencies are the Departments of Agriculture, Commerce, Defense, Education, Energy, Health and Human Services, Homeland Security, Housing and Urban Development, the Interior, Justice, Labor, State, Transportation, the Treasury, and Veterans Affairs; the Environmental Protection Agency, General Services Administration, National Aeronautics and Space Administration, National Science Foundation, Nuclear Regulatory Commission, Office of Personnel Management, Small Business Administration, Social Security Administration, and U.S. Agency for International Development.

[43] A control deficiency exists when the design or operation of a control does not allow management or employees, in the normal course of performing their assigned functions, to prevent or detect and correct misstatements on a timely basis.

[44] See Pub. L. No. 107–347, Dec. 17, 2002; 44 U.S.C. 3541, et seq.

[45] GAO, *Cybersecurity: National Strategy, Roles, and Responsibilities Need to Be Better Defined and More Effectively Implemented*, GAO–13–187 (Washington, DC: Feb. 14, 2013).

[46] See, most recently, Department of Homeland Security, *NIPP 2013: Partnering for Critical Infrastructure Security and Resilience.*

[47] H.R. 3696, 113th Cong. (2013).

DHS to, among other things, establish a voluntary program to support the adoption of a cybersecurity framework by private-sector partners;[48] coordinate the establishment of a set of incentives designed to promote participation in the voluntary program; and incorporate privacy and civil liberties protections into every initiative called for by the Executive Order.

Securing Federal Systems

In carrying out its role in overseeing and assisting Federal agencies in implementing information security requirements, DHS has begun performing several activities. These include:
- conducting "CyberStat" reviews, which are intended to hold agencies accountable and offer assistance in improving their information security posture;
- holding interviews with agency chief information officers and chief information security officers on security status and issues;
- establishing a program to enable Federal agencies to expand their continuous diagnostics and mitigation capabilities; and,
- refining performance metrics that agencies use for FISMA reporting purposes.

In February 2014, as part of our continued dialogue with DHS regarding progress and what remains to be accomplished in this high-risk area, we identified and communicated to DHS actions critical to addressing its efforts to oversee and assist agencies in improving information security practices.[49] This included the following:
- *Expand CyberStat reviews to all major Federal agencies.*—DHS has conducted CyberStat sessions with several of the 24 major Federal agencies. According to DHS officials, the current approach focuses on providing CyberStat reviews for the lowest-performing agencies. However, expanding the reviews to include all 24 agencies could lead to an improved security posture.
- *Enhance FISMA reporting metrics.*—In September 2013, we reported that the metrics issued by DHS for gauging the implementation of priority security goals and other important controls did not address key security activities and did not always include performance targets.[50] We recommended that OMB and DHS collaborate to develop improved metrics, and the agencies stated that they plan to implement the recommendation by September 2014.
- *Develop a strategic implementation plan.*—DHS's Office of Inspector General reported in June 2013 that the Department had not developed a strategic implementation plan describing its cybersecurity responsibilities and a clear plan of action for fulfilling them. According to DHS officials, it has developed this plan and is awaiting closure of the inspector general recommendation. We will review the status of this plan as part of our on-going review of this high-risk area.
- *Continue to develop continuous diagnostics and mitigation capabilities and assist agencies in developing and acquiring them.*—This effort is intended to protect networks and enhance an agency's ability to see and counteract day-to-day cyber threats.

The successful implementation of these actions should result in outcomes such as enhanced DHS oversight and assistance through CyberStat, improved metrics and other outcomes, improved situational awareness, and enhanced capabilities for assisting agencies in responding to cyber incidents. In conjunction with needed actions by Federal agencies, this could contribute to improved information security Government-wide.

Protecting Cyber Critical Infrastructure

DHS, in conjunction with other Executive branch entities, has taken steps to enhance the protection of cyber critical infrastructure. For example, according to DHS, it has:
- expanded the capacity of its National Cybersecurity and Communications Integration Center to facilitate coordination and information sharing among Federal and private-sector stakeholders;
- established the Information Sharing Working Group and a mechanism for creating cyber threat reports that can be shared with private-sector partners; and,

[48] As required by Executive Order 13636, the National Institute of Standards and Technology (NIST) issued the first version of the cybersecurity framework in February 2014. See NIST, *Framework for Improving Critical Infrastructure Cybersecurity*, Version 1.0 (Feb. 12, 2014).

[49] We provided DHS detail on the actions that need to be taken and outcomes that need to be achieved to address the Federal information security and cyber critical infrastructure protection high-risk area. The information we provided DHS was based on our full body of work in this area.

[50] GAO, *Federal Information Security: Mixed Progress in Implementing Program Components; Improved Metrics Needed to Measure Effectiveness*, GAO–13–776 (Washington, DC: Sept. 26, 2013).

- set up a voluntary program to encourage critical infrastructure owners and operators to use the cybersecurity framework developed by the National Institute of Standards and Technology, as required by Executive Order 13636.

In February 2014, we identified and communicated to DHS actions critical to addressing cyber critical infrastructure protection, including the following:

- expand the Enhanced Cybersecurity Services program, which is intended to provide Classified cyber threat and technical information to eligible critical infrastructure entities, to all critical infrastructure sectors as required by Executive Order 13636;
- enhance coordination efforts with private-sector entities to facilitate improvements to the cybersecurity of critical infrastructure; and,
- identify a set of incentives designed to promote implementation of the NIST cybersecurity framework.

Completing these efforts could assist in achieving a flow of timely and actionable cybersecurity threat and incident information among Federal stakeholders and critical infrastructure entities, adoption of the cybersecurity framework by infrastructure owners and operators, and effective implementation of security controls over a significant portion of critical cyber assets. As we reported in March 2014, more needs to be done to accelerate the progress made in bolstering the cybersecurity posture of the Nation and Federal Government. The administration and Executive branch agencies need to implement the hundreds of recommendations made by GAO and agency inspectors general to address cyber challenges, resolve known deficiencies, and fully implement effective information security programs. Until then, a broad array of Federal assets and operations will remain at risk of fraud, misuse, and disruption, and the Nation's most critical Federal and private-sector infrastructure systems will remain at increased risk of attack from our adversaries.[51]

Enhancing the Sharing of Terrorism-Related Information

DHS has made significant progress in enhancing the sharing of information on terrorist threats and in supporting Government-wide efforts to improve such sharing.[52] Our work on assessing the high-risk area on sharing terrorism-related information has primarily focused on Federal efforts to implement the Information Sharing Environment, as called for in the Intelligence Reform and Terrorism Prevention Act of 2004.[53] The Information Sharing Environment is a Government-wide effort to improve the sharing of terrorism-related information across Federal agencies and with State, local, territorial, Tribal, private-sector, and foreign partners. When assessing progress, we review the activities of both the program manager for the Information Sharing Environment—a position established under the 2004 Act with responsibility for information sharing across the Government—as well as efforts of DHS and other key entities, including the Departments of Justice, State, and Defense, and the Office of the Director of National Intelligence.[54] Accordingly, DHS itself is not on the high-risk list nor can DHS's efforts fully resolve the high-risk issue. Nevertheless, DHS plays a critical role in Government-wide sharing given its homeland security missions and responsibilities.

Overall, the Federal Government has made progress in addressing the terrorism-related information-sharing high-risk area. As we reported in our February 2013 update, the Federal Government is committed to establishing effective mechanisms for managing and sharing terrorism-related information, and has developed a National strategy, implementation plans, and methods to assess progress and results. While progress has been made, the Government needs to take additional action to mitigate the potential risks from gaps in sharing information, such as ensuring that it is leveraging individual agency initiatives to benefit all partners and continuing work to develop metrics that measure the homeland security results achieved from improved sharing. We are currently conducting work with the program manager and key entities to determine their progress in meeting the criteria since the 2013 high-risk report.

---

[51] GAO, *Government Efficiency and Effectiveness: Views on the Progress and Plans for Addressing Government-wide Management Challenges*, GAO–14–436T (Washington, DC: March 12, 2014).

[52] Terrorism-related information includes homeland security, terrorism, and weapons of mass destruction information. See 6 U.S.C. §§ 482(f)(1), 485(a)(1), (5)–(6).

[53] See Pub. L. No. 108–458, § 1016, 118 Stat. 3638, 3664–70 (2004) (codified as amended at 6 U.S.C. § 485).

[54] The Office of the Director of National Intelligence was established in 2004 to manage the efforts of the intelligence community. See 50 U.S.C. § 3023. Its mission is to lead intelligence integration and forge an intelligence community that delivers the most insightful intelligence possible.

DHS's Role in the Sharing of Terrorism-Related Information

Separately, in response to requests from this committee and other Congressional committees, we have assessed or are currently assessing DHS's specific efforts to enhance the sharing of terrorism-related information. As discussed below, this work includes DHS efforts to: (1) Support State and major urban area fusion centers,[55] (2) coordinate with other Federal agencies that support task forces and other centers in the field that share information on threats as part of their activities, (3) achieve its own information-sharing mission, and (4) share information related to the Department's intelligence analysis efforts.

Fusion centers.—A major focus of the high-risk area and Information Sharing Environment has been to improve the sharing of terrorism-related information among the Federal Government and State and local security partners, which is done in part through State and major urban area fusion centers. DHS is the Federal lead for supporting these centers and has made significant strides. For example, DHS has deployed personnel to centers to serve as liaisons to the Department and help centers develop capabilities (such as the ability to analyze and disseminate information), provided grant funding to support center activities, provided access to networks disseminating Classified and Unclassified information, and helped centers identify and share reports on terrorism-related suspicious activities. DHS has been very responsive to a recommendation in our 2010 report that calls for establishing metrics to determine what return the Federal Government is getting for its investments in centers.[56] We have an on-going review of DHS's efforts to assess center capabilities, manage Federal grant funding, and determine the contributions centers make to enhance homeland security, and expect to issue a report later this year.

Field-based entities that share information.—DHS is also taking steps to measure the extent to which fusion centers are coordinating and sharing information with other field-based task forces and centers—such as Federal Bureau of Investigation Joint Terrorism Task Forces—and assess opportunities to improve coordination.[57] In April 2013, we reported that fusion centers and other field-based entities had overlapping activities, but the agencies that support them had not held the entities accountable for coordinating and collaborating or assessed opportunities to enhance coordination, and recommended that the agencies develop mechanisms to do so.[58] In response, DHS began tracking collaboration mechanisms, such as which fusion centers have representatives from the other entities on their executive boards, are co-located with other entities, and issue products jointly developed with other entities.

DHS's efforts can help avoid unnecessary overlap in activities, which in turn can help entities leverage scarce resources. To fully address our recommendation, however, the other Federal agencies must take steps to better hold their respective field entities accountable for such collaboration. In addition, these agencies must work with DHS to collectively assess Nation-wide any opportunities for field entities to further implement collaboration mechanisms.

DHS information-sharing mission.—In September 2012, we reported that DHS had made progress in achieving its own information-sharing mission, but could take additional steps to improve its efforts.[59] Specifically, DHS had demonstrated leadership commitment by establishing a governance board to serve as the decision-making body for DHS information-sharing issues. The board has enhanced collaboration among DHS components and identified a list of key information-sharing initiatives to pursue, among other things. We found, however, that 5 of DHS's top 8 priority initiatives faced funding shortfalls. We also reported that DHS had taken steps to track its information-sharing efforts, but had not fully assessed how such efforts had improved sharing. We recommended that DHS: (1) Revise its policies and guidance

---

[55] In general, fusion centers are collaborative efforts of two or more agencies that provide resources, expertise, and information to the center with the goal of maximizing their ability to detect, prevent, investigate, and respond to criminal and terrorist activity. See 6 U.S.C. § 124h(j)(1). There are 78 fusion centers in the United States.

[56] GAO, *Information Sharing: Federal Agencies Are Helping Fusion Centers Build and Sustain Capabilities and Protect Privacy, but Could Better Measure Results*, GAO–10–972 (Washington, DC: Sept. 29, 2010).

[57] The five types of entities we reviewed are State and major urban area fusion centers, Joint Terrorism Task Forces, Field Intelligence Groups, Regional Information Sharing Systems Centers, and High-Intensity Drug Trafficking Area Investigative Support Centers. DHS, the Department of Justice, and the Office of National Drug Control Policy oversee or otherwise support these entities.

[58] GAO, *Information Sharing: Agencies Could Better Coordinate to Reduce Overlap in Field-Based Activities*, GAO–13–471 (Washington, DC: Apr. 12, 2013).

[59] GAO, *Information Sharing: DHS Has Demonstrated Leadership and Progress, but Additional Actions Could Help Sustain and Strengthen Efforts*, GAO–12–809 (Washington, DC: Sept. 18, 2012).

to include processes for identifying information-sharing gaps; analyzing root causes of those gaps, and identifying, assessing, and mitigating risks of removing incomplete initiatives from its list, and (2) better track and assess the progress of key initiatives and the Department's overall progress in achieving its information-sharing vision. DHS has since taken actions—such as issuing revised guidance and developing new performance measures—to address all of these recommendations.

Sharing intelligence analysis. We are finalizing a report on DHS's intelligence analysis capabilities, which are a key part of the Department's efforts in securing the Nation. Within DHS, the Office of Intelligence and Analysis has a lead role for intelligence analysis, but other operational components—such as CBP and ICE—also perform their own analysis activities and are part of the DHS Intelligence Enterprise. Our report, expected to be issued later this month, will address: (1) The extent to which the intelligence analysis activities of the enterprise are integrated to support Departmental strategic intelligence priorities, and are unnecessarily overlapping or duplicative; (2) the extent to which Office of Intelligence and Analysis customers report that they find products and other analytic services to be useful, and what steps, if any, the office has taken to address any concerns customers report; and (3) challenges the Office of Intelligence and Analysis has faced in maintaining a skilled analytic workforce and steps it has taken to address these challenges. We are planning to make recommendations to help DHS enhance its intelligence analysis capabilities and related sharing of this information.[60]

Overall, DHS's continued progress in enhancing the sharing of terrorism-related information and responding to our findings and recommendations will be critical to supporting Government-wide sharing and related efforts to secure the homeland.

Chairman McCaul, Ranking Member Thompson, and Members of the committee, this completes my prepared statement. I would be happy to respond to any questions you may have at this time.

Chairman MCCAUL. Well, thank you, sir. We thank you for your comments as well.

Chairman now recognizes Mr. Roth.

STATEMENT OF JOHN ROTH, INSPECTOR GENERAL, U.S. DEPARTMENT OF HOMELAND SECURITY

Mr. ROTH. Good morning, Chairman McCaul, Ranking Member Thompson, and Members of the committee. Thank you for inviting me here today to discuss some of the high-risk areas that DHS faces.

My testimony here today will focus on acquisition management. In particular, as our work has shown, DHS is not as effective and efficient as it could be in this area. We find that it stems from three main areas.

First, DHS's unique mission requires complicated acquisitions. Whether it is acquiring a fleet of helicopters, building a border fence over hundreds of miles of varied terrain, integrating and managing systems from diverse legacy agencies, or purchasing technologically-complex airport screening machines are, under the best of circumstances, high-risk acquisitions.

Second, DHS, as has been noted this morning, is working towards a transparent acquisition governance process, which if it is fully followed would lead to better and smarter acquisitions. Unfortunately, the DHS components engaged in the acquisitions often do not follow the DHS procurement policies, and DHS lacks a means to enforce compliance.

Third, components acquisition decisions often work against the Department's stated goal of One DHS. DHS components, in a word, operate in a vacuum. They fail to take into account other compo-

---

[60] The Office of Intelligence and Analysis' five customer groups are: (1) DHS leadership; (2) DHS operational components; (3) intelligence community members; (4) State, local, Tribal, and territorial partners; and (5) private critical infrastructure sectors.

nents' needs or they fail to leverage other assets or other acquisitions that are already underway.

We have done a number of audits that give examples of this. Those are in my written testimony. But I would like just to talk about one single audit that we did with regard to using acquisitions to have One DHS.

DHS's stated goal is to ensure interoperability of communications. We want to make sure that the first responders and other law enforcement agencies—agents, particularly within DHS, can talk to each other through a common channel in the event of a terrorist event or a crisis of some sort.

DHS has about 123,000 radio field users within eight different components, and DHS has invested about $430 million in equipment, infrastructure, and other resources to ensure interoperability.

We conducted an audit in late 2012 and asked 479 DHS field radio users to access and use the specified channel to communicate. Out of those 479 people we asked to do so, only a single user could use the common channel.

In other words, DHS had a failure rate of 99.8 percent. Seventy-two percent of the users didn't even realize that there was—didn't even know the existence of a common channel. The remainder just couldn't find it. Of the radios we examined only 20 percent of them were properly set up to use the common channel.

This test happened 11 years after 9/11. Without an effective governing structure DHS cannot achieve its goal of a Department-wide radio interoperability. As we sit here today the Department's plans to do so are still a work in progress.

In closing I would like to note that DHS has taken steps to implement our recommendations and to progress towards a unity of effort. However, the Department is persistently challenged in acting in an integrated single entity.

This concludes my prepared statement. I am happy to take questions from the committee. Thank you.

[The prepared statement of Mr. Roth follows:]

PREPARED STATEMENT OF JOHN ROTH

MAY 7, 2014

Good morning Chairman McCaul, Ranking Member Thompson, and Members of the committee. Thank you for inviting me here today to discuss high-risk areas at DHS identified by GAO.

In its report, *High-risk Series: An Update* (GAO–13–283, February 2013), GAO identified high-risk areas in the Federal Government, including areas of particular concern at DHS. My testimony today will focus on some high-risk areas that we also identified in our December 2013 report, *Major Management and Performance Challenges Facing the Department of Homeland Security* (OIG–14–17), particularly in managing acquisitions.

Our work has shown that DHS' management of its acquisitions is not as effective and efficient as it could be. This problem stems from three main issues:

- First, DHS' unique mission requires multi-faceted and sophisticated acquisitions. Whether acquiring a fleet of helicopters, building a border fence over hundreds of miles of varied terrain, or integrating and managing systems from diverse legacy agencies, DHS' requirements increase the complexity and risk of its acquisitions.
- Second, DHS is working toward a transparent, authoritative governing process—the Acquisition Life-cycle Framework (ALF)—which, if fully implemented, would lead to better oversight and guidance of acquisitions. Unfortunately, DHS

components often do not follow this governing process (or any other) in carrying out their acquisitions, and DHS has had difficulty enforcing compliance.
- Third, the components' acquisition decisions often work counter to the Department's stated goal of "One DHS." In planning and managing acquisitions, components often operate in a vacuum; they fail to take into account the needs of other components or they fail to leverage other assets or acquisitions already underway.

We have made recommendations to improve the efficiency and effectiveness of DHS' programs and operations, and DHS has taken some steps to implement our recommendations. However, the Department continues to struggle with acting as an integrated, single entity to accomplish its mission.

NATURE OF THE RISK

Acquisition management at DHS is inherently complex and high-risk. It is further challenged by the magnitude and diversity of the Department's procurements. In fiscal year 2013, DHS' Major Acquisition Oversight List included 123 programs; 88 (72 percent) of the programs were Level 1 or Level 2. Level 1 and Level 2 programs have life-cycle costs of $300 million or more or have special Departmental interest. Some examples of Level 1 and Level 2 acquisitions include:
- The United States Coast Guard's HC–144A Maritime Patrol Aircraft, a twin engine turboprop airplane designed for superior situational awareness, a reduced workload, and increased crew safety. Life-cycle cost estimate—$24.9 billion;
- U.S. Customs and Border Protection's (CBP) Automated Commercial Environment, a system to enable CBP to interact, manage, and oversee import and export data, and manage custodial revenue and enforcement systems. Life-cycle cost estimate—$4.5 billion;
- TSA's Screening Partnership Program, procures screening services from private companies at TSA airports. Life-cycle cost estimate—$2.4 billion;
- CBP's Mission Support Facilities to develop, plan, execute, and sustain facilities and infrastructure inventory to support CBP's Mission Support Offices Nationwide. Facilities include administrative offices, training centers, laboratories, and warehouses. Life-cycle cost estimate—$2 billion;
- CBP's Integrated Fixed Towers, a system for automated, persistent wide area surveillance to detect, track, identify, and classify illegal entries. Life-cycle cost estimate—$842 million.

COMBATING THE RISK: ACQUISITION MANAGEMENT FRAMEWORK

Effective acquisition management requires careful planning and oversight of processes, solid internal controls, and compliance with laws and regulations. Acquisitions must be planned and managed through their entire life cycle to ensure that they are procured, deployed, and used efficiently and effectively.

DHS has developed a comprehensive acquisition framework of policies, procedures, and entities to streamline its acquisition practices and ensure that procured goods and services meet mission needs cost-efficiently. This system should lead to informed investment decisions on goods and services that fulfill DHS' mission.

Acquisition Phases

DHS has adopted the Acquisition Life-Cycle Framework (ALF), composed of the following four phases, to determine whether to proceed with an acquisition:
    1. Need—identify the need that the acquisition will address;
    2. Analyze/Select—analyze the alternatives to satisfy the need and select the best option;
    3. Obtain—develop, test, and evaluate the selected option and determine whether to approve production; and
    4. Produce/Deploy/Support—produce and deploy the selected option and support it throughout the operational life cycle.

Each phase of the ALF leads to an "Acquisition Decision Event" (ADE), a predetermined point at which the acquisition is reviewed before it can move to the next phase. The reviews are intended to ensure alignment of needs with DHS' strategic direction and adequate planning for upcoming phases.

The figure below shows the four phases of the ALF and each ADE.

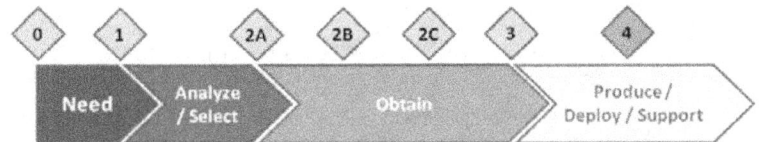

ADE–0 Identify the need
ADE–1 Validate the need
ADE–2A Approve the program
ADE–2B Approve projects within the program
ADE–2C Approve low rate initial production
ADE–3 Approve full rate production and deployment
ADE 4* Project transition—a milestone unique to the Coast Guard, authorizes the project to move to sustainment

The ALF is a rigorous, disciplined process designed to result in cost-efficient acquisitions that can meet the Department's needs and help accomplish its mission.

Acquisition Entities, Policies, and Procedures

DHS' Office of Program Accountability and Risk Management (PARM) administers the ALF and oversees all major DHS acquisitions. PARM reports directly to the under secretary for management and manages and implements the Department's Acquisition Management Directive. PARM is also responsible for independently assessing major investment programs and monitoring programs between formal reviews to identify issues.

DHS has established the following mechanisms to govern acquisitions:
- *The Acquisition Review Board (ARB).*—A cross-component board composed of senior-level decisionmakers. The ARB determines whether a proposed acquisition meets requirements and can proceed to the next phase and eventual production and deployment. Before every ADE, components must submit acquisition documents to the ARB for review, including a mission needs statement, capability development plan, and an acquisition plan.
- *Quarterly Program Accountability Report.*—Provides a comprehensive, high-level analysis of a program's vital signs provided to DHS leadership, component acquisition executives, and program managers.
- *A Joint Requirements Council.*—Reviews high-dollar acquisitions and recommends savings opportunities to the ARB.
- *Centers of Excellence.*—Two have been set up under PARM: Program Management Center of Excellence and Cost Estimating & Analysis Center of Excellence. Leadership staff and subject-matter experts at the centers provide proven practices, guidance, and counsel on program management and cost estimating and analysis.
- *The Decision Support Tool.*—A web-based central dashboard to assess and track the health of major acquisition projects, programs, and portfolios. The Department's goal is to improve program accountability and make sound strategic decisions throughout the life-cycle of major acquisitions.
- *Comprehensive Acquisition Status Report.*—Provides information on the status of major acquisitions. Reports include information such as the current acquisition phase, the date of last review, life-cycle cost estimate, and key events and milestones.

FAILING TO FOLLOW THE FRAMEWORK RESULTS IN PROBLEMATIC ACQUISITIONS

However, as our work has shown, this process is not always followed. Several of our audits have highlighted DHS' challenge in establishing an overarching structure that fully integrates the components into overall governance, unified decision making, and collective analysis.

CBP's Acquisition of H–60 Helicopters

In May 2013, we issued *DHS' H–60 Helicopter Programs (Revised)* (OIG–13–89), which illustrates the risks of deviating from the ALF. Although the Department had some processes and procedures to govern its aviation assets and provide oversight, the acquisition was not fully coordinated and acquisition costs, schedules, and performance were not controlled.

CBP did not take into account guidance from the DHS Office of the Chief Procurement Officer (OCPO) in its H–60 acquisition planning. In 2007, CBP's Office of Air and Marine submitted its Congressionally-mandated acquisition plan, which outlined how its aviation assets and acquisitions would support its mission. CBP leadership approved the plan to acquire 38 new and converted medium-lift helicopters and submitted it to the DHS OCPO.

On March 3, 2008, OCPO expressed its concerns about the program in a memo to CBP. According to OCPO, CBP needed to address substantive issues in the acquisition plan. CBP should have had two separate H–60 plans, and both should move independently through the acquisition review process, including ARB review. OCPO was also concerned that CBP—

- Had not clearly defined the acquisition's period of performance;
- Did not have a complete life-cycle cost estimate;
- Had not completed a cost-benefit analysis to compare upgrading its existing fleet to purchasing new helicopters; and
- Had not used various contracting best practices.

Just 3 days after receiving the memo from OCPO, CBP nevertheless continued with the H–60 acquisition by signing an agreement with the U.S. Army.

In March 2010, the ARB concluded that both CBP and the Coast Guard were pursuing H–60 conversions and directed the Coast Guard to collaborate with CBP, report on possible helicopter program synergies, and present a joint review within 75 days. The Coast Guard was not able to complete the review because CBP did not provide the needed information.

Subsequent attempts to push the acquisition into the ALF failed.

We recommended that DHS direct CBP to apply all ALF requirements to all its aviation-related acquisitions. DHS concurred with this recommendation, and CBP was directed to submit its plans to acquire aviation assets to PARM. According to DHS, the ARB would review and decide on CBP's aviation programs and projects as they progressed through the ALF.

Information Technology Investments

In August 2012, we issued *CBP Acquisition of Aviation Management Tracking System (Revised)* (OIG–12–104). We reported that although CBP had a joint strategy to unify its aviation logistics and maintenance system with those of the Coast Guard, it planned to purchase a new, separate system. This system would not be coordinated with the Coast Guard's already operational system. We concluded that the acquisition did not comply with the Secretary's efforts to improve coordination and efficiencies among DHS components. Acquiring the new system would also be a continuation of components' past practices of obtaining disparate systems that cannot share information. If CBP instead transitioned to the Coast Guard's system, it would improve tracking of aviation management and cost less than purchasing a new system.

DHS Governance of Aviation Assets

DHS historically has had little formal structure to govern the Department's aviation assets and no specific senior official to provide expert independent guidance on aviation issues to DHS senior management. The Department has intermittently issued policies and established various entities to oversee its aviation assets and operations, but it has not sustained these efforts. For example, DHS set up an Aviation Management Council in 2005, but oversight was inconsistent, and the council stopped meeting in 2007. In 2009, Department-level oversight of DHS' aviation assets resumed. An Aviation Issue Team led by the Office of Program Analysis and Evaluation reviewed potentially co-locating component aviation facilities, finding commonality in component aviation assets, and combining component aviation-related information technology systems.

In 2011, the deputy secretary established an Aviation Working Group, but the group did not have a charter, defined roles and responsibilities, or an independent aviation expert. It collected data on CBP and USCG missions, aircraft inventories, flight hours, and aviation resources; reviewed components' funding plans and opportunities for joint acquisitions; and considered an organizational structure for a Department-wide aviation office. However, according to senior officials, without an authoritative expert, DHS was relying on unverified information from components to make aviation-related decisions.

In addition to challenges in establishing a structure to govern aviation assets, DHS has had difficulty bringing aviation-related acquisitions into the ALF. For example, CBP's Strategic Air and Marine Plan (STAMP) has an estimated life-cycle cost of about $1.5 billion. STAMP encompasses all of CBP's aviation-related acquisitions used to detect, interdict, and prevent acts of terrorism near and across or across U.S. borders. CBP does not believe that STAMP should be subject to the ALF because the program existed before DHS established the framework. We contend (and have recommended) that individual programs and projects under STAMP should go through the ALF separately.

Unmanned Aircraft

In CBP's *Use of Unmanned Aircraft Systems in the Nation's Border Security* (OIG–12–85, May 2012), we reported that CBP had not adequately planned the resources needed to support its unmanned aircraft. CBP's plans to use the unmanned aircraft did not include processes to ensure that: (1) Each launch and recovery site had the required operational equipment; (2) stakeholders submitted mission requests; (3) mission requests were prioritized; and (4) it obtained reimbursement for missions flown on stakeholders' behalf. Because these were not included, CBP risked having invested substantial resources in a program that underutilized resources and limited its ability to achieve its mission goals. Specifically, our audit showed that CBP had not achieved its scheduled or desired levels of flight hours for the unmanned aircraft. We estimated that 7 unmanned aircraft should support 10,662 flight hours per year to meet the minimum capability and 13,328 flight hours to meet desired capability. However, staffing and equipment shortages, coupled with FAA and other restrictions, limited actual flight hours to 3,909—37 percent of the unmanned aircraft's mission availability threshold and 29 percent of its mission availability objective.

CBP's Advanced Training Center Acquisition

In February 2014, we issued *U.S. Customs and Border Protection's Advanced Training Center Acquisition* (OIG–14–47). We reported that CBP did not effectively oversee and manage the fourth phase of the acquisition of its Advanced Training Center. Although not subject to the ALF, CBP did not comply with Federal and Departmental regulations governing acquisitions. CBP did not develop and execute the $55.7 million agreement with its service provider, the U.S. Army Corps of Engineers, according to Federal, Departmental, and component requirements. In particular, CBP did not develop, review, or approve a required independent Government cost estimate and acquisition plan prior to entering into the agreement. Key documentation supporting the agreement with the Corps of Engineers was either missing or incomplete. CBP also approved millions of dollars worth of contract modifications to the agreement without first ensuring the need and reasonableness of the modifications. In addition, CBP improperly used reimbursable work authorizations to transfer money for this project, as well as other construction projects. During our audit, CBP began taking action to ensure future compliance with all statutory requirements; CBP concurred with all our recommendations.

TSA's Advanced Imaging Technology

We issued *Transportation Security Administration's Deployment and Use of Advanced Imaging Technology (Revised)* (OIG–13–120) in March 2014. We reported that the Transportation Security Administration (TSA) did not develop a comprehensive deployment strategy for using advanced imaging technology (AIT) units—procured at a cost of nearly $150 million—at airports. Because TSA did not have reliable data to determine whether the units were effectively deployed, TSA decision makers could not implement efficiency improvements.

This occurred because TSA did not have a policy or process requiring program offices to prepare strategic acquisition or deployment plans for new technology that aligned with the overall goals of the Passenger Screening Program.

The AIT units did not undergo a stand-alone acquisition review, but were instead reviewed as part of the Passenger Screening Program. Because the AIT units met the Level 1 acquisition threshold, they should have gone through all the steps required for that level. TSA should also have developed a deployment strategy for the AIT units, but it only developed a deployment schedule.

Without documented, approved, and comprehensive plans, as well as accurate data on the use of AIT, TSA continued to screen the majority of passengers with walkthrough metal detectors. This potentially reduced AIT's security benefits, and TSA may have used resources inefficiently to purchase and deploy AIT units that were underused.

FAILING TO USE ACQUISITIONS TO FORGE "ONE DHS"

In addition to failing to manage high-risk acquisitions through a governing process, DHS acquisitions often miss opportunities to ensure DHS acts in a concerted and efficient manner. DHS has struggled to become fully integrated. With 22 components and a range of missions, cooperation, and coordination continue to be a challenge. The Department's structure sometimes leads to "stovepiping"—components operating independently and management often not cooperating and sharing information to benefit "One DHS." In an April 2014 memorandum for DHS leadership, the Secretary reiterated the need to strengthen the Department's "unity of effort."

During our recent audits, we identified several programs in which there was little or no cross-component coordination and communication and weak Department-level authority. These led to cost inefficiencies and ineffective program management. Therefore, we made recommendations to enhance collaboration to improve both efficiency and effectiveness and prevent waste and abuse.

DHS Radio Equipment Program

DHS manages about 197,000 pieces of radio equipment and 3,500 infrastructure sites, with a reported value of more than $1 billion. We issued a pair of reports that highlighted the problematic nature of some of the acquisition processes for communications equipment.

In one of our audits, *DHS' Oversight of Interoperable Communications* (OIG–13–06, November 2012), we tested DHS radios to determine whether DHS components could talk to each other in the event of a terrorist event or other emergency. They could not. Only 1 of 479 radio users we tested—or less than one-quarter of 1 percent—could access and use the specified common channel to communicate. Further, of the 382 radios tested, only 20 percent (78) contained all the correct program settings for the common channel. In other words, DHS components could not talk to each other using $430 million worth of radios purchased nearly a decade after the 9/11 Commission highlighted the problem. They could not do so because DHS did not establish an effective governing structure with the authority and responsibility to ensure it achieved Department-wide, interoperable radio communications. We also reported that without an effective governing structure and a concerted effort to attain interoperability, the Department's progress would remain limited.

DHS' plans to achieve interoperability are still in progress. The Department has drafted, but not finalized, a DHS Communications Interoperability Plan; it has extended the date of signature from April to September of this year.

In August 2013, we issued *DHS Needs to Manage Its Radio Communication Program Better* (OIG–13–113). We reported that without sound investment decisions on radio equipment and supporting infrastructure, DHS could not effectively manage its radio communication program. DHS had not implemented a governance structure with authority to establish policy, budget and allocate resources, and hold components accountable for managing radio programs and related inventory. Components were still independently managing their current radio programs with no formal coordination with the Department. They used different systems to record and manage personal property inventory data, including radio equipment. The components' inventory data also indicated they did not record radio equipment consistently in personal property systems. As a result, DHS was making management and investment decisions for the radio communication program using inconsistent, incomplete, and inaccurate real and personal property data.

We concluded that a Department-wide inventory would help DHS prioritize its needs, plan its investments, and help plan future acquisitions and manage communication networks. DHS also needs a strong governance structure over its radio communication program. Thus, we recommended that the Department develop a single portfolio for radio equipment and infrastructure and establish a Department-level point of accountability. In response to our recommendations, DHS said that because of budget constraints, it would include a time line and resources for portfolio management in its fiscal year 2016 Resource Allocation Plan. The Department was collecting data to develop a single profile of assets, infrastructure, and services; reviewing existing policies and procedures; and planning to revise its personal property manual by June 30, 2014.

Cross-Border Tunnel Program

In our audit of CBP's and U.S. Immigration and Customs Enforcement's (ICE) efforts to monitor and detect illegal cross-border tunnels (*CBP's Strategy to Address Illicit Cross-Border Tunnels,* OIG–12–132, September 2012), we reported that although CBP is creating a program to address capability gaps in countering the cross-border tunnel threat, it had not demonstrated how its detection strategy would consider ICE's needs.

CBP and ICE need coordination and oversight in developing these technologies because the Border Patrol's mission objective is to prevent illegal traffic from crossing the border while ICE's objective is to investigate and dismantle criminal organizations.

Without taking into account both components' needs, the Department risks not being able to disrupt criminal organizations that engage in cross-border smuggling.

We made recommendations to improve consideration of CBP's and ICE's needs and to improve DHS' coordination and oversight of counter-tunnel efforts.

CBP took action on our recommendations, including formation of an Integrated Product Team, which includes relevant stakeholders. It also planned to draft required acquisition planning documents and submit the program to the ARB.

Aviation

Our audit of CBP's H–60 helicopter program showed that CBP did not properly oversee and manage the conversion and modification of its H–60 helicopters, which affected the cost-effectiveness and timely delivery of the converted and modified H–60s. We noted that increased cooperation between CBP and the Coast Guard in managing the conversion and modification of its H–60 helicopters would reduce redundancies and potentially save millions of dollars. Specifically, if CBP were to complete the conversions and modifications at a Coast Guard facility, it would save about $126 million and H–60s would fly 7 years sooner. The Department's own independent study confirmed that CBP would realize substantial savings by using the Coast Guard facility. Specifically, DHS estimated CBP could save at least $36 million and as much as $132 million in the cost of conversion alone. According to DHS, it could not be more precise because CBP did not provide sufficient data.

Mr. Chairman, this concludes my prepared statement. I welcome any questions you or other Members of the committee may have.

APPENDIX

Major Management and Performance Challenges Facing the Department of Homeland Security, OIG–14–17, December 2013
Independent Auditors' Report on DHS' FY 2013 Financial Statements and Internal Control over Financial Reporting, OIG–14–18, December 2013
DHS' H–60 Helicopter Programs (Revised), OIG–13–89, May 2013
U.S. Customs and Border Protection's Management of the Purchase and Storage of Steel in Support of the Secure Border Initiative, OIG–12–05, November 2011
Transportation Security Administration's Deployment and Use of Advanced Imaging Technology, OIG–13–120, March 2014
DHS Needs to Manage Its Radio Communication Program Better, OIG–13–113, August 2013
United States Customs and Border Protection's Radiation Portal Monitors at Seaports, OIG–13–26, January 2013
DHS' Oversight of Interoperable Communications, OIG–13–06, November 2012
CBP's Strategy to Address Illicit Cross-Border Tunnels, OIG–12–132, September 2012
CBP's Use of Unmanned Aircraft Systems in the Nation's Border Security, OIG–12–85, May 2012
Unclassified Summary of Information Handling and Sharing Prior to the April 15, 2013 Boston Marathon Bombings, April 10, 2014
DHS Uses Social Media to Enhance Information Sharing and Mission Operations, But Additional Oversight and Guidance Is Needed, OIG–13–115, September 2013
DHS Can Make Improvements to Secure Industrial Control Systems, OIG–13–39, February 2013
CBP's and USCG's Controls Over Exports Related to Foreign Military Sales, OIG–13–118, September 2013
U.S. Customs and Border Protection Has Taken Steps to Address Insider Threat but Challenges Remain, OIG–13–118, Redacted, September 2013
DHS Needs to Strengthen Information Technology Continuity and Contingency Planning Capabilities, OIG–13–110, Redacted, August 2013
DHS Can Take Actions to Address its Additional Cybersecurity Responsibilities, OIG–13–95, June 2013
DHS' Efforts to Coordinate the Activities of Federal Cyber Operations Centers, OIG–14–02, October 2013
Homeland Security Information Network Improvements and Challenges, OIG–13–98, June 2013

Chairman MCCAUL. Thank you, Mr. Roth.

The Chair now recognizes himself for 5 minutes.

Mr. Mayorkas, let me first commend you for the clean audit, for getting more items off the high-risk list, for your efforts in DHS acquisition. The memo that came out recently by you and the Secretary actually mirrors our legislation that we passed unanimously out of committee. So I do commend you for that.

But I do have to raise an issue that happened last Thursday when the Secretary of Homeland Security placed the former acting inspector general, Mr. Edwards, under leave after a Senate report came out alleging among other things that Mr. Edwards intentionally changed and withheld information in some IG reports to accommodate the administration's political appointees, and that he sought outside legal advice, compromising the IG's independence.

Now, I don't know if these allegations are accurate. But if they are, this is the internal watchdog. This is sort-of like the old adage the fox guarding the henhouse.

I know you are concerned about this, as I am. But can you tell me, has the Department launched an investigation into these allegations?

Mr. MAYORKAS. Thank you very much, Mr. Chairman. I would like to make two points in response to your very important question, one specific to the announcement to which you refer last Thursday.

That is that the Secretary took swift and strong action in placing the former inspector general on administrative leave, and made the very important point that as additional facts are learned, appropriate action will be taken. So this is a matter that is under process. I don't think it would be appropriate for me to speak in more depth about a personnel matter.

The overarching point that I would like to make is the following, and it is a very simple but a very important message. That is that the highest degree of ethics and integrity are conditions of employment in the Department of Homeland Security.

Chairman MCCAUL. So after this came out the Secretary placed him on administrative leave and the inspector general has been tasked to investigate the current inspector general, who is with us today. Is that correct or not?

Mr. MAYORKAS. I am actually not certain as to who is conducting that investigation, Mr. Chairman. Perhaps my colleagues here know.

Chairman MCCAUL. Leads me to my next question. Mr. Roth, are you investigating these allegations?

Mr. ROTH. We are not. What we have is within the Inspector General Act a process by which allegations against either the inspector general or people within reporting to the inspector general, allegations with regard to misconduct get investigated.

There is the entity called the Committee of IGs for Integrity and Efficiency that has a special investigative committee. They have received a complaint—a series of complaints really, with regard to the former acting inspector general.

That has now been farmed out to a different inspector general to ensure objectivity and you know to ensure that it is an independent and objective review of that. My understanding is that that investigation is being conducted by the inspector general from the Department of Transportation.

Chairman MCCAUL. Because these allegations are so serious the decision was made not to go with the IG within DHS, but rather farm it out to the IG at the Department of Transportation.

Mr. ROTH. That is correct. Again, we followed the Inspector General Act, which basically dictates how these things should work.

Chairman MCCAUL. I mean does it concern you about these allegations involving allegations out of Cartagena with the Secret Service, or a report for $650,000 that was never disclosed on accountability and risk management?

Mr. ROTH. It deeply concerns me. Essentially the morning after I read the report I ordered that those reports be taken down from our public website.

I have tasked a senior lawyer from our Office of General Counsel, that is our Office of General Counsel, not the Department's Office of General Counsel, to conduct an internal investigation to talk to the career auditors who actually researched and wrote those reports to find out exactly what was changed, why it was changed, to restore those reports to its original condition and then repost it and report the results of it, not only to the committee but to the public.

Chairman MCCAUL. Well, we look forward to hearing the results of that investigation. I also appreciate your testimony about the lack of interoperability at a 99.8 percent failure rate, which is astounding to me.

The final question to Mr. Dodaro, and that is you mentioned information sharing with respect to terrorism threats and cybersecurity, two issues very important to me and to this committee. After the Boston report have you done an analysis of the failure of information sharing?

Mr. DODARO. No, we have not been asked to take a look at that particular situation.

Chairman MCCAUL. But you still mention that is high-risk in the DHS list.

Mr. DODARO. Oh yes, definitely. It looks at not only DHS but the five other—or four other agencies that are involved. It is a Government-wide high-risk designation in terms of information sharing.

DHS is an important part of it. But we do look at the program manager at the DNI, the Director for National Intelligence, as well as the coordination with the Treasury and Justice and DHS.

Chairman MCCAUL. Of course we know the inspector generals for the ICE and Department of Justice and DHS all came out with their report, which was, I think, a very candid assessment about what happened that day and what failed that day.

With that, the Chairman now recognizes the Ranking Member.

Mr. THOMPSON. Thank you, Mr. Chairman.

Following that line of questions from the Chairman, Mr. Dodaro, do you foresee any time in the near future that DHS will get off the high-risk list?

Mr. DODARO. I think there is ample opportunity for continued progress. They need to meet the criteria for coming off the list, particularly getting another year of a clean opinion on the financial statements, but also on internal controls.

There is a statutory requirement that they have an opinion on internal controls, which is rather unique in the Federal Government, but nonetheless it is there and their current time frame for doing that and modernizing their financial systems is 2016 and beyond.

They need to also demonstrate that they need to—that they can bring some of these acquisitions in within budget, scheduled on time and deliver a functionality that was originally intended by those acquisitions.

So you know those are only two areas. I mean there are milestones within the other ones as well. So I think it is achievable in a relatively short-term, but it is going to take a while to actually produce these results.

I am committed to working with the Department constructively. But I am not going to take anything off the high-risk list until the problems have been resolved.

Mr. THOMPSON. Well, you referenced some material weaknesses within Coast Guard, FEMA, ICE, and CBP. What has been the response from those agencies when you shared those weaknesses with them?

Mr. DODARO. They have listened to what we have had to say. But there needs to be agreement not only in the Department—within the components, excuse me, but also at the Department-wide level.

I mean part of the time that has been lost there in the financial management systems, which is what I was specifically talking about, is the Department pursued two efforts at least to have a Department-wide financial management system. Both of those efforts failed. Now they have tried to have a component-oriented approach to doing this, which can work, but it needs to have Department leadership.

So we are going to be looking more carefully at this financial management modernization effort that they have under way. But it is still in its early stages. FEMA is the one that is furthest behind.

Mr. THOMPSON. To the extent, Mr. Roth, you kind-of highlighted some of this in terms of the acquisitions and other things we have experienced within DHS. Explain what—you said that somehow DHS is in charge but that the components don't follow the regulations.

I think you were saying we have DHS up here and we have got these other people under here and the people down here kind-of do what they want to do. The people up top just kind-of observe them. So, who is really in charge?

Mr. ROTH. That is exactly the issue that we see. I mean right now the Department has something called the Acquisition Life-Cycle Framework, which is a, sort-of a framework that is there to ensure that acquisitions are well thought-out, that there are trigger points for review by high-level Department officials to ensure that we are spending money in the right way.

It is a good program. It is run by the under secretary for management in a group called the Program Accountability and Risk Management Section within the under secretary's office. It works when it is used because it is deliberate. It is objective. It allows money to be spent in the right way.

The difficulty is it was only set up in 2011. So you have some of these very high-dollar acquisitions.

For example, the Customs' Air and Marine program, basically the ships and the helicopters and the airplanes that Customs purchases, all high-risk acquisitions, all big-dollar acquisitions, something like $1.5 billion life-cycle costs for these things, are not part of that system because they pre-existed.

What we believe ought to happen is that the leadership, the Secretary and the deputy secretary need to, candidly, be firmer with the components to ensure that these kinds of acquisitions get forced into the framework that DHS has set up.

Mr. THOMPSON. I yield back.

Chairman MCCAUL. Chairman recognizes Dr. Broun from Georgia.

Mr. BROUN. Thank you, Mr. Chairman.

Let me wish Mr. Dodaro a happy birthday myself too. So I hope you have a great day, sir. It is a great way to spend it is with us.

Mr. DODARO. Well, I am ending it on the Senate.

Mr. BROUN. Well, I wish you well over there too. I think we are nicer than they are over there.

But my first question to you guys is that we have, as Members of this committee, struggled with the jurisdiction issues. It seems to me that when any entity has multiple bosses then they have absolutely nobody in charge and no true boss.

I am concerned about where we are going. We look at the high-risk issues and what is happening with acquisition and with cyber-security and with all the other areas that you all have brought forward as being problem areas.

I will start with Mr. Dodaro. Would you comment as to the issue of jurisdiction? Is this—is jurisdictional problems part of why the DHS is struggling so much and has all these high-risk areas? If so, what would you recommend? How would you recommend to rectify that?

Mr. DODARO. I don't believe jurisdictional issues are a factor in these high-risk designations, particularly with management functions within the Department. I think it is just a matter of the Department having to get the processes in place and execute properly.

I mean in many cases they have the right policies in place. They are just not executing them appropriately. It is just a matter of the Department having to work more to provide guidance to the components and use the power of the purse, if you will, to not let them spend money unless they have approved baselines for acquisitions and they have done proper testing.

I mean they shouldn't be able to move forward without that. I mean the prescription for success in this area is very clear in following best practices. But they are just not following it.

You could—you know, the jurisdictional issues I don't believe are at play here. It is just a manner of good management and follow-through and discipline.

Mr. BROUN. So this is a management problem then within the Department itself?

Mr. DODARO. Yes, for the management areas on the high-risk list definitely.

Mr. BROUN. How far up the chain does that go as far as management problems?

Mr. DODARO. Well, I think it goes to the highest levels in the——

Mr. BROUN. As far as the Secretary?

Mr. DODARO. Yes. I think everybody has to be engaged. I think the Secretary's memo that he just announced in April to have more integrated planning and budgeting and requirements management and putting structures in place in the environment that work effectively would be a great step forward if they can get that done.

Now, in the other areas in the cybersecurity and the information-sharing area, those are Government-wide high-risk areas. So the Department itself can't address those issues.

Theirs were I don't think jurisdictional issues at play, but it requires broader oversight by the Congress because it is a Government-wide area. Those areas I think some joint hearings and some other efforts with other committees that have responsibility, and the House and Senate working together would be helpful, particularly in passing legislation, which we have called for to clarify DHS's role and responsibilities as it relates to Federal oversight of computer security and critical infrastructure protection.

There I think you need more parts of the Congress working together to help DHS get the proper authorities in place.

Mr. BROUN. Well, you say it is a Government-wide problem and overall in some of those areas. But that is not an excuse though that one department, DHS, which we have jurisdiction over shouldn't be solving that problem. Is that correct?

Mr. DODARO. Oh, that is absolutely correct. We have been looking at whether DHS even within the Department is sharing information. We have a report that will be coming out soon on the Office of Intelligence Analysis as to whether or not DHS, within its own organization, is sharing information properly. That is exactly right, Congressman Broun.

Mr. BROUN. Mr. Roth, do you have any comment on acquisition just very quickly? I have got 30 seconds left to my time. So if you would be expeditious in your answer.

Mr. ROTH. I think Mr. Dodaro summed it up. We know what to do. We know the process that can be used to make smarter, better acquisitions. The question is forcing the components to follow that process.

Mr. BROUN. This is a long-standing problem. This is not just with this current Secretary or the past Secretary. It has been really ever since it has been stood up is my understanding. Is that correct?

Mr. ROTH. That is correct. Again, this process was only stood up in 2011 to try to integrate everything under the under secretary.

Mr. BROUN. Very good. Thank you, Mr. Chairman. My time is expired.

Chairman McCAUL. Thank you. Just to follow up my colleague's comments, when we are talking about jurisdiction though in the Congress, not within the Department but within the Congress, when the Secretary has to report to over 100 committees and subcommittees, doesn't that detract from the core mission of protecting the American people, Mr. Dodaro?

Mr. DODARO. Well, we have not looked at that issue. But it is not uncommon in many departments and agencies for the Department of Defense, for example, to have multiple committees to report to.

I think early on, and I am going back to the creation of the Department, there wasn't enough transparency in working with the Congress and having open communication. That I think fostered a set of relationships that have to be overcome, and are being overcome over a period of time.

So I think if there was more transparency and the Department was actually producing the plans, the jurisdictional issues wouldn't be as acute as they have been because of that I would say getting off on the wrong foot in its relationship with the Congress.

Chairman MCCAUL. Well, again, this is not an issue I fault the Department on. I actually fault the Congress on this one because we can't pass any legislation without multiple referrals to multiple committees.

It becomes dysfunctional within the Congress. Then it takes time and attention away from senior leadership that need to be doing their job to report to over 100 committees and subcommittees. The Aspen Institute came out with a report talking about it.

We need to—it was one of the top recommendations of the 9/11 Commission was to have the DHS report to a single oversight committee. That recommendation has never been followed by Congress. I think we need to change that.

I am a little disappointed in the answer. I think Mr. Mayorkas may disagree with you on that. Do you?

Mr. MAYORKAS. Mr. Chairman, I think the Secretary has addressed you and other Members of the Congress expressing his deep concern with respect to the jurisdictional issue and the position it places the Department in.

Chairman MCCAUL. It detracts from the core mission. With that, the Chairman now recognizes Mr. Richmond from Louisiana.

Mr. RICHMOND. Thank you, Mr. Chairman.

Mr. Dodaro, now I want to talk about the National Flood Insurance Program. I see that you have made several comments or recommendations regarding it. Do you have any concerns that their current capacity or these notations that you made will affect their implementation of the new Homeowner Flood Insurance Affordability Act?

Mr. DODARO. I think there are a number of recommendations that we have made, for example in modernizing their claims management system that need to be put in place. The implementation of the Act will be a new challenge for them that could detract from some of the implementation of these recommendations.

But I think it is very important for them to continue their efforts to modernize the claims system and oversee the contractors that write the policies for the Flood Insurance Program.

Mr. RICHMOND. Well, that is exactly where I wanted to go because you used the term the reasonableness of compensation to the insurance companies that sell and service most of the NFIP policies. Do we think their compensation is on the unreasonable side in terms of high or low? Or is it something that we need to look into?

Mr. DODARO. You definitely need to look into that issue. I mean I think that that is an important question and that is something that we think requires more oversight and whether or not the compensation is appropriate.

Mr. RICHMOND. Our numbers, and I don't know if your numbers would say the same things, in that through the life of the Flood Insurance Program that the amount of money in premiums that have gone in almost equals the amount of money that is going out, except that you have all the administrative expenses that any insurance company would have.

But everywhere we can reduce those administrative costs or the costs that the insurance companies are charging for either servicing or the commissions that they receive, we make the program more stable. We can directly save the taxpayers money on those. Have you looked at——

Mr. DODARO. Yes. I think the administrative costs need to be under constant review to make sure that they are at the minimum necessary to operate the program. However, the premiums in our opinion have not been sufficient to cover the costs of the programs.

I mean currently the National Flood Insurance Program owes the Treasury $24 billion and hasn't made a principal payment since 2010 on that issue. So it is not really actuarially sound going into the future. So that is one of the reasons it is on the high-risk list.

Mr. RICHMOND. Right. I don't think that we will ever get to actuarially sound and maintain a sense of affordability for the 5 million homeowners who participate in the program.

But I think the goal should be that where we can save money we should save money. Where we can be more efficient we should be more efficient. So that is my concern when we talk about the efficiency of the management of the program and making sure that the people who service the program are being as efficient, and we are very diligent in terms of what we are paying them.

So the other thing you mentioned was the debt management and how that could offer us some cost savings.

Mr. DODARO. Well, I think it is important that they figure out how to both build a reserve for the future potential cost, but also how to figure out how to repay the Treasury Department for the amount of money that they owe. That is going to be a tall order for them given the current statutory framework on which they have to operate under.

So I think additional action will be needed by the Congress to help them in order to put the program on a firmer financial footing.

Mr. RICHMOND. Then I guess we can have the whole philosophical debate. But we have to get it on firm financial footing. But actuarial rates is probably not the way to do it considering that many of these homes were built before there was a requirement for flood insurance. To go back and change it in our area we saw rates increasing from $500 and $600 to $10,000 a year, which will cause another mortgage collapse and all of those things.

Mr. DODARO. So I agree with you. I think—I mean there has to be a balance between affordability and fiscal responsibility and accountability and in this case transparency because if the homeowners aren't paying for the insurance that means the general taxpayers are. It is not really clear what the subsidies are. I am particularly concerned about the future.

We have put also on the high-risk list limiting the Federal Government's exposure by better managing climate change risks. With the potential for climate change and other additional issues in the offing, I mean this program is one that requires I think constant scrutiny and more transparency about who is paying for what in the program.

But I agree with you, affordability has to be a policy priority.

Mr. RICHMOND. Mr. Chairman, I see my time is expired. I was just going to ask Mr. Mayorkas if he had a response. I am not requiring one.

Mr. MAYORKAS. I do not. I do not, Mr. Congressman.

Mr. RICHMOND. Thank you, Mr. Chairman. Yield back.

Mr. MAYORKAS. Mr. Chairman, may I make a point if I may, even though there is no question pending to me I feel compelled to share something with the committee because my colleagues have expressed concern that components do not necessarily follow the direction that a best practice would require to address a management challenge.

I think it is very important to communicate to this committee very clearly to ensure that there is no misimpression that the components are willfully disobeying guidance. It is not an issue of that. But it is rather an issue of putting the structures and the mechanisms in place to drive everyone in the same direction and to ensure a disciplined and rigorous adherence to best practices. It is really a matter of accountability.

I know there was a reference made that we don't have appropriate accountability mechanisms in place, and I would respectfully disagree with that. Quite frankly, if there is a failure of a component to adhere to a best practice in the service of addressing a management challenge, I am ultimately accountable for that.

Of course the Secretary is. But I am overseeing the management of the Department on behalf of the Secretary, and that accountability regime rests with me.

Chairman MCCAUL. Well, I appreciate you taking responsibility for that. I hope to see some good results.

Chairman recognizes Mr. Duncan.

Mr. DUNCAN. Thank you, Chairman, for this valuable hearing today. I want to thank the panelists for the comments that they made about H.R. 4228 and the acquisition reform bill.

You know the goal is to improve discipline accountability and transparency and acquisition program management and a lot of things that I am hearing on all the topics today come down to just those basic disciplines of doing best practices and all of the acquisition reform.

So I heard Secretary—I mean Comptroller Dodaro say this. But deputy secretary, have you had a chance to review H.R. 4228?

Mr. MAYORKAS. I have, sir.

Mr. DUNCAN. Okay. Do you believe it will aid DHS in addressing acquisition management challenges?

Mr. MAYORKAS. I do, sir. I should inform you and this committee that in reviewing the proposed legislation that this committee passed I have drawn some practices that we should adopt and not await the passage of the legislation.

Mr. DUNCAN. Thank you. I agree. Whether we have to have Congressional legislation passed or not it is the right thing for the Department to do. I think the Secretary agrees with us as well. So thanks for saying that.

With the most recent GAO high-risk report citing the Department's continued management challenges, and with our country being $17.5 trillion in debt, do you think it is wise for DHS to continue to spend scarce spending on unnecessary green initiatives and costly renovations on a project such as St. Elizabeth's that won't be complete until 2026, and will cost the American taxpayer about $4.5 billion or more, deputy secretary?

Mr. MAYORKAS. Mr. Congressman, as a general principle of course no expenditure of funds should be permitted that does not yield an effective and efficient delivery of service on behalf of the American people.

The Secretary is reviewing the St. Elizabeths project, and we are as a Department with all components involved taking a look at what our resource investment should be in light of the cost and our current budget environment. It was as recently as yesterday that all the components met with the Secretary and me on that very subject.

Mr. DUNCAN. Well, I think that is great. I appreciate the Secretary reviewing that. I just don't believe that—you know in a utopian society rainwater flush toilets are awesome.

But when you are $17.5 trillion in debt and you are accountable to every taxpayer dollar, I think you need to start questioning that and maybe the use of the hardest wood from Brazil for the decking when you could use a composite material that will last just as long and save the taxpayer dollars. So I appreciate your efforts and I look forward to that.

I ask the comptroller general about St. Elizabeths and the cost overruns. I know GAO has looked at that. Do you care to comment on saving taxpayer dollars and that?

Mr. DODARO. Well, certainly we support the effort to do any program activity at the least cost possible. We are currently looking at the St. Elizabeths situation and we will be happy to share our report with this committee as soon as it is complete.

Mr. DUNCAN. We look forward to that as well.

So deputy secretary, given the large number of programs still lacking Department-approved documents and experiencing cost overruns and schedule delays, what do you believe is the biggest challenge with regard to the high-risk list, the biggest challenge in doing effective oversight of DHS major acquisition programs?

Throw out some challenges that you have got. There might be another nugget in there that we can pursue from the Congressional side.

Mr. MAYORKAS. Thank you, Mr. Congressman. I think that my colleagues Mr. Dodaro and Mr. Roth have identified issues with respect to our acquisition program.

The Secretary, through the Unity of Effort memorandum that he issued, to which the Chairman referenced, puts in place a structure to drive better acquisition oversight and management. I lead under the Unity of Effort, a paradigm, I lead the deputy's Management Action Group where we are all—components and headquarters—together in ensuring that capabilities are identified, the needs are properly identified.

The gaps are therefore disclosed. We don't close those gaps without establishing effective requirements, understanding our budget constraints, being effective and efficient in the use of our money, and ensuring that the delivery of service takes all of those factors into account.

Mr. DUNCAN. I am about out of time. I will say that hearings like this are refreshing.

What I am hearing from all the gentlemen is that it seems that the Department is moving in the right direction. I would attribute the Chairman's leadership and this committee for helping nudge the Department in the right direction with regard to acquisition management and addressing a lot of the concerns that were brought about by the gentleman from Louisiana and the gentleman from Georgia.

So I want to applaud the Department for continuing to move in that direction. I can tell you we are going to be right behind you to make sure that the trend continues.

With that, Chairman, I yield back.

Chairman MCCAUL. We also commend your leadership as Chairman of the Oversight Subcommittee. You have done a fantastic job.

Chairman recognizes Mr. O'Rourke from Texas.

Mr. O'ROURKE. Thank you, Mr. Chairman. I would like to present the panel with two current acquisition projects and then get your comments.

The first is one that we had a hearing on within the last month, the Arizona Border Surveillance Technology Plan, which essentially would spend between $500 million to $700 million to put a series of fixed towers along the Arizona-Mexico border with a high-tech surveillance system there, obviously to try to apprehend people who might cross into the country illegally.

This is on the heels of the failed SBInet program that spent a billion dollars and achieved almost nothing at great taxpayer cost and Government waste. In that hearing we learned from someone on your team at the GAO that there were several significant findings that the GAO had made, including no clear metrics and no clear life-cycle costs for that program. So that is one that comes to mind.

The second in El Paso, Texas is a half-mile stretch of currently unfenced border between El Paso and Juárez, an area where in the last 4 years without there being a fence total crossings have dropped year after year and they are at a fraction of what they were even 4 or 5 years ago.

It is also a very historical crossing point. Don Juan De Onate in the 16th Century crossed there.

The sensitivity is so great that not only have I but the other Congressman representing the area, one of our U.S. Senators, the city council, the State senators, the State delegation have all pleaded with CBP not to construct that wall there at a cost of $5.5 million. But we were told by the acting commissioner at the time that the wheel is already in motion and it is too hard to stop this.

So with those two examples my question is: When is it an appropriate time to put on the brakes? I would think that those major findings that the GAO made after the failure of SBInet we should stop before proceeding with this Arizona Border Surveillance Technology Initiative.

The $5.5 million in El Paso may not sound like a lot, but $5.5 million here, $5.5 million there soon it adds up and becomes real money. So I would like to get your thoughts on how we get greater control on spending when there are findings, when there are concerns raised by this committee or the GAO, when it might be appropriate to pause and rethink some of those projects.

Mr. Mayorkas, we will start with you.

Mr. MAYORKAS. Thank you very much, Congressman. I have, in the short time that I have been in office I have visited the Texas-Mexico border as well as the Arizona-Mexico border. I will tell you that visiting—there is no substitute for visiting the border because one understands first-hand the challenges that it presents.

The lesson that I learned there is certainly it is not a one-size-fits-all model. There have to be different technological and operational solutions to address the very different and very diverse challenges that the Southwest Border presents.

You ask a very fact-specific question, which is: When is it right to pull out of a project when the project isn't going well? I think that——

Mr. O'ROURKE. Not just pausing the project. We could use Arizona—the border surveillance plan there. Would it not make sense for DHS to stop spending until those GAO concerns are resolved?

Mr. MAYORKAS. Congressman, as a general matter I find it untenable to continue to pour money into a project when one doesn't have a level of confidence in the effectiveness and efficiency of the undertaking. So that is a general principle.

In fact we have executed on that general principle over the last few months. We have paused. We have suspended discrete projects because we have not had confidence in the stability of the undertaking.

So there is no shyness. There is no hesitation to do that in order to make sure that we do not develop something that is ineffective by the time it is deployed——

Mr. O'ROURKE. Right.

Mr. MAYORKAS [continuing]. And we create more work for our oversight——

Mr. O'ROURKE. Sorry to interrupt, but I have little time left. You have paused in other projects. Will you pause in this project?

Mr. MAYORKAS. I—as I sit here today, Mr. Congressman, I am not aware of a reason why the Integrated Fixed Towers Project should be paused. I will tell you that is——

Mr. O'ROURKE. I gave you two.

Mr. MAYORKAS. I will have to look into the second one, which is the wall that——

Mr. O'ROURKE. I gave you two reasons on that Arizona Border Surveillance. No life-cycle costs and no clear metrics for what that is supposed to achieve after spending up to $700 million.

Could I hear from Mr. Dodaro on this and Mr. Roth if there is time?

Mr. DODARO. Yes. Our report focused on the fact their cost estimates and the schedule estimates weren't complete or reliable. There was limited testing planned on there as well as the fact that there weren't metrics tying it to the particular problem.

The Department agreed with most of the recommendations. Except I was disappointed they didn't agree to do more testing on this. I think this is important given the past history and some of those other activities.

So I think it is important that these issues be addressed before they proceed into full-scale production.

Mr. O'ROURKE. If the Chairman will allow, I would love to hear from Mr. Roth on this, if you have any comments.

Mr. ROTH. Yes. The entire life-cycle—acquisition life-cycle framework requires in fact certain stopping points where an examination is done by independent senior leadership to ensure that it should go forward in a timely way or in a rational way.

So there are stop points all the way along, and it is perfectly appropriate during an acquisition to hold off and address concerns.

Mr. O'ROURKE. Okay. Thank you.

Thank you, Mr. Chairman.

Chairman MCCAUL. Chairman recognizes Mr. Sanford from South Carolina.

Mr. SANFORD. I thank the Chairman. I apologize for getting here late. So I did not get to hear the entirety of your testimony. I was caught up in another meeting.

But I jotted in a note in looking at preliminary brief. There was a GAO report that said, DHS could better manage its portfolio, address funding gaps and improve communication with Congress.

One of the findings was basically that there was a gap between acquisition of programs and the overall Homeland Security strategy. That at several different junctures this gap was seen between acquisition and strategy.

I have got a quote here. I am beginning to lose my eyesight. But it says "GAO goes on to say in its report that none of the reports that DHS put out consistently identified how individual acquisition programs would help DHS to achieve its goals." Then there is some more verbiage from there.

So I guess I would turn to the GAO, to you, Mr. Dodaro. Thoughts on that? What else did you see with regard to this gap between a time strategy and individual acquisition programs?

Mr. DODARO. There really are two types of gaps. One is the one that you mentioned. But the second is a funding gap issue in terms of whether or not you have enough money there. I mentioned earlier in my opening statement that of the major acquisitions, 46% don't have approved baseline costs and 77% don't have life-cycle costs.

Now, even with that limitation the Department undertook an effort a year or 2 ago to identify what the gap would be if all these acquisitions would cost certain amount of money and the Department had certain amount of resources. They have figured that there was 30% gap between what these acquisitions will cost and what they were likely going to have money for, which means they need to set priorities.

Of course in setting priorities you have to go with what your overall strategies are and what kind of priorities are in your strategy. So they need a governance structure at the Department to set these priorities across the Department because they are not going to have, you know, enough money to be able to deal with these issues.

This is a similar issue we brought to the Department of Defense's attention. It will particularly be true if sequestration resumes in 2016 through 2022.

So it is very important that they deal with this. I know they have some plans to do it. But they are in the very early stages.

Mr. SANFORD. Couldn't it be said of pretty much any Government agency that there is always a gap between what they would like to have and what they would get? I mean so isn't that——

Mr. DODARO. Well——

Mr. SANFORD. I mean it may——

Mr. DODARO. Well, but——

Mr. SANFORD [continuing]. The issue within Homeland Security or DOD, but——

Mr. DODARO. Right.

Mr. SANFORD [continuing]. That seems to be a consistent refrain.

Mr. DODARO. Well, there is a difference between what you—how much money you are going to have and what you would like to have a lot of money, as opposed to how many projects you have already started down the road that you are not going to be able to complete.

That is a different situation. I am saying in that case they are spending money to get these projects up and running, and they are not going to have enough to finish, the money, so that those projects that aren't finished will be not optimal use of the taxpayers' money.

As opposed to, we are not going to have this amount of money, here is the priority we want to do. We need to stop this acquisition or we need to redirect our funds to other areas.

So it is very important to do that, particularly given the rather poor track record that they have in delivering their acquisitions with functionality, within cost and on time.

Mr. SANFORD. If you were just waving a magic wand and as you look at this agency in particular, are there other things that perhaps didn't make your report but things that entered your mind? Or that you all evaluated but found too controversial and maybe left off, where you would say this is an area of opportunity that Homeland Security ought to look at in terms of better optimizing taxpayer dollar in maybe a way that they aren't?

Mr. DODARO. No. I think our report is pretty complete. I mean we put everything out there that we have identified.

Since the Department has been created we have made over 2,000 recommendations to the Department. About 65% of them they have implemented. They have efforts underway in other areas to implement.

So we—I think we have been pretty thorough in pointing out all the major areas that need attention.

Mr. SANFORD. I suspect you might have a counterpoint to some of this and I therefore would offer the floor to you in the few seconds that I have got left.

Mr. MAYORKAS. Congressman, I think I actually will not have a counterpoint. I think, quite frankly, that the work of Mr. Dodaro and his team has helped make us better, and identified gaps that we need to fill. I think I can say the same for the work of Mr. Roth and his team.

You used the word opportunity. Fortunately I am an optimist and so I look at the challenges we have as opportunities, opportunities to be better.

Mr. Dodaro referred to the fact that a governance structure presents some hope, some cause for optimism, but it is at the nascent stage. That is true.

Both the Secretary and I are new. The Secretary has put in place a governance structure and we will drive to achieve its aspiration.

Mr. SANFORD. I burned through my time. Thank you, Mr. Chairman. Yield back.

Chairman MCCAUL. Chairman recognizes Mr. Payne.

Mr. PAYNE. Thank you, Mr. Chairman.

Mr. Roth, you know the findings in the November 2012 IG report on interoperable communications at DHS are very concerning. I have introduced legislation to DHS Interoperable Communications Act that aims to address the problems, you know, related to the Government structure and strategy identified in the report.

In your testimony you mentioned that the Department has developed but not finalized DHS Communications and Interoperability Plan. Have you seen drafts of this plan?

Mr. ROTH. I have.

Mr. PAYNE. Okay. What do you think to this point?

Mr. ROTH. We made our primary recommendation after doing the audit that had the 99.8% failure rate, was that there ought to be an interagency structure that had an individual or group with true power to be able to require the components to get interoperable systems.

The Department, inexplicably in my mind, non-concurred with that, and instead went forward with what we consider to be a lesser proposal requiring essentially cooperation among the components.

We think that is the wrong way to go. We think showing strong leadership is the way to go, and essentially forcing compliance by the components.

Mr. PAYNE. Yes. Well, you know it is clear based on information I have that this legislation, you know, is crucial to finally get Department-wide interoperability.

I was shocked to hear that in your testimony, you know in your test case, only 1 out of 479 first responders were able to get on a common channel. You know 1 out of 479.

What is it going to take to achieve interoperability? As you say, the Department is obviously not following recommendations that have been made. That you say have decided to go with a lesser plan. What is it going to take to get to interoperability?

Mr. ROTH. Well, certainly hearings like this I think highlight the problem. Accountability by this committee and other committees and the American people to ensure that the purposes behind DHS, which was to have all these disparate agencies under one roof so they could in fact talk to each other is a good thing.

But again, it is a promise that has not yet been kept.

Mr. PAYNE. Okay. You said many didn't even know that the common channel existed. Is it going to take more training or as you said more hearings like this and a concerted effort on us to push them in that direction?

Mr. ROTH. To be fair, this test took place in 2012 before the current administration within DHS was appointed. We are hearing good things from the Secretary and the deputy secretary with regard to unity of effort.

I am optimistic that we can get there. But I am frankly concerned that as we speak today a Secret Service agent in New York can't get on his radio and talk to a Federal Protective Service officer in New York or a CBP officer in El Paso can't talk to a Homeland Security Investigations Agent in the same city.

Mr. PAYNE. Okay.

Thank you, Mr. Chairman. I yield back.

Chairman MCCAUL. Let me just state for the record, Mr. Payne, your bill on interoperability will be part of our mark-up in May coming up soon. So we thank you for that.

Chairman now recognizes the gentlelady from New York, Ms. Clarke.

Ms. CLARKE. Thank you, Mr. Chairman. Thank you, Ranking Member.

My first question is to you, Mr. Mayorkas. I want to talk about the Department's transition to a large portion of its information technology to the cloud, and a couple of questions with regard to that.

Does the CIO work with the Department cybersecurity and privacy experts to ensure that proper protections are in place for cloud-based technologies? How does this improve efficiency?

Do you anticipate this move to the cloud resulting in cost savings? What steps are being taken to ensure that the private cloud utilized by the Department is secure?

Mr. MAYORKAS. Thank you very much, Congresswoman, for the question. The answer is yes.

The head of information technology, Luke McCormack, does work very closely with our NPPD, our directorate, and Susanne Spaulding. It is made to ensure that the use of the cloud passes cyber-hygiene, if you will.

What the cloud provides is the ability for the Department to essentially pull on an as-needed basis certain technological capabilities. So with that nimbleness and surgical use of IT not only do we gain effectiveness, but we also gain cost savings.

Ms. CLARKE. Well, there has been a lot of talk here on the Hill. We have turned our attention to immigration reform and proposals such as the DREAM Act may create a pathway for many millions of youngsters becoming American citizens. This could create a major influx of applications coming to the USCIS system.

Would the limitations of current paper-based system that I am sure you know all too well, how will USCIS handle this increased caseload? Are there any activities underway at the headquarters level to address this impending issue?

Mr. MAYORKAS. Thank you very much for that question, Congresswoman. We of course remain committed to comprehensive immigration reform. I think there are two streams of activity that are responsive to your question.

One is to develop the technological capabilities to accept a large influx of new applicants in an electronic or on-line environment. That effort is under way. It is a very significant and challenging effort, but we are making progress in it. It is called transformation to move from a paper-based agency to an on-line environment on the one hand.

On the other hand, U.S. Citizenship and Immigration Services, which I was very proud to be a part of for 4 years, is extraordinarily adept at handling surges in the number of individuals coming before it. It has exhibited that nimbleness and that adeptness in the last 2 years in taking on a huge surge in previously unanticipated applicants.

Ms. CLARKE. So you believe that the transformative nature of the new technologies that you are currently sort-of testing would be able to manage potentially, you know, tens of thousands if not millions of individuals seeking to apply for—through for immigration reform and the personnel commensurate with that is sort-of trained and gearing up as well?

Mr. MAYORKAS. Congresswoman, the goal of transformation is to be able to do that. We are working towards that. It is a challenging undertaking, but we are working towards that on the one hand.

On the other hand, to be able to address an increase in applications of, for example, 11.5 million people, there is an infrastructure that needs to be built. We have communicated very clearly to the bipartisan committee that passed the Senate bill last year.

They understood and legislated accordingly that there needs to be some ramp-up time so that the agency could in fact build the infrastructure to take on that significant new workload. But not just personnel, but facilities, IT infrastructure and the like, but we are prepared with time and funding to meet that challenge.

Ms. CLARKE. Very well. Then I just wanted to quickly—my time is winding down—talk about disciplinary practices. There are a lot of folks who believe that there are some—it is inequitable and oftentimes arbitrary.

For example, there is no Department-wide standard for penalties. The same offense can engender different results without any sound reason for this discrepancy.

Would you agree that the Department could benefit from standardized disciplinary processes? How not having these processes in place can have an impact on low morale, for instance?

Is a Department-wide standard for penalties under consideration? If not, why?

Mr. MAYORKAS. That is a very interesting question, Congresswoman. When I was the director of U.S. Citizenship and Immigration Services, we actually had that infirmity within the agency that we did not have really a cohesive and consistent discipline regime, and we implemented one during the course of my tenure.

Whether there should be a Department-wide standard is a question that I would actually like to give thought to because I will tell you that there are different dynamics at play within each component of the Department. There are different unions, union leadership, union relationships.

I think at a general level my immediate reaction is that we should have standardized processes and we should have consistency in the response—in the disciplinary response to similar behaviors. I would like to actually give further study, and quite frankly speak with my colleagues here to my left with respect to your question.

Ms. CLARKE. My time is run out, but if the Chairman gives another round, we will——

Chairman MCCAUL. Well, if you would like to hear other witnesses——

Ms. CLARKE. Oh, certainly.

Chairman MCCAUL. This is our final round.

Ms. CLARKE. Okay. Thank you, Mr. Chairman.

Well then, gentlemen, would you please give me your opinion on these disciplinary actions?

Mr. ROTH. Thank you. We have not done an audit with regard to this except with the Secret Service, which did not have a table of penalties. We found that that was a problematic issue with regard to some of the issues that occurred in the Secret Service.

I think I would join Mr. Mayorkas in indicating that that is a broader issue that we would probably need to study in a more thoughtful way.

Mr. DODARO. Yes. We have looked recently at TSA employee misconduct issues and how that is handled. I would be happy to provide that for the record and any other thoughts that we have on this matter.

Ms. CLARKE. Very well. I appreciate that, gentlemen. Thank you all for your testimony here today.

Thank you, Mr. Chairman. I yield back.

Chairman MCCAUL. Thank you. I want to thank the witnesses.

Chairman recognizes the Ranking Member.

Mr. THOMPSON. I just want to thank the Chairman for this hearing and the witnesses for their candid comments in response to the questions.

The thing that continues to bother me, though, is we put the Department of Homeland Security under one roof. But it just appears that there are some outliers within the Department that continue to do as they please.

We have reports after reports that continue to highlight those do-as-you-please efforts that cost money. What I have taken away is that you continue to highlight it, but somehow it doesn't get implemented.

I guess I am struggling for—can you, each one of you witnesses provide us in writing what you think it would take for the Department to run seamlessly, all the components within DHS using one standard for procurement and other things?

Right now procurement, personnel, a lot of issues continue to be different. I think if we have One DHS, if we have this now Unity of Effort approach, how can we actually accomplish that if we still have Coast Guard, FEMA, CBP, ICE kind-of doing what they want to do? I am just kind-of concerned about that, that we should just have a standard system.

Now, obviously there are some exceptions. But I think those exceptions can be noted. But I would like to see something from our witnesses since they have been so good that could help give this committee some direction on how we can come up with one system, whether it is IT system or whatever, in those categories that have been outlined.

I yield back.

Chairman McCaul. I concur with the Ranking Member. We would like to see that, if you could respond maybe in writing after the hearing.

I know Ms. Clarke and I have worked on the iCloud concept in terms of bringing the One DHS together. I think that is an interesting concept as well.

I did have one last question for Mr. Roth. The Secret Service has mentioned, know you are reviewing your predecessor's report, the allegations involving drunkenness during Presidential protection. Very serious concern on the part of this committee that that conduct is still on-going within Secret Service.

I know you are reviewing those currently. When do you anticipate that your report will come out?

Mr. Roth. We are looking at the current reports. We are not engaged in a further audit or inspection of that. But what we are doing is in light of the Senate subcommittee's report we are looking to ensure that any of the conclusions within the report were untainted by any sort-of political or other improper considerations.

We are doing that as expeditiously as possible, but we want to get it right. I am hopeful in the next few weeks we will be able to get it out. But right now I can't give you——

Chairman McCaul. Will you be providing any guidance to the director of the Secret Service in terms of—you mentioned there are no real sort of disciplinary procedures in place.

Mr. Roth. At the time of our audit there were no disciplinary procedures. There were no tables of penalties. That has been fixed.

In the series of audits we did, we did a look-back to see what the internal investigation looked like. We also did what was known as the so-called culture report.

In the culture report we had a series of recommendations that we asked the Secret Service to do. They are in the process of complying with each of those. I am happy to give a interim report as to, sort-of, how they are doing with regard to responding to our recommendations.

Chairman McCaul. I would appreciate that. Protecting the President is one of the highest duties——

Mr. Roth. Yes.

Chairman McCaul [continuing]. Within the Department.

So we thank the witnesses for testifying here today. The record will be open for 10 days. You may have additional questions. With that, without objection, committee stands adjourned.

[Whereupon, at 11:31 a.m., the committee was adjourned.]

APPENDIX

QUESTIONS FROM CHAIRMAN MICHAEL T. MCCAUL FOR ALEJANDRO N. MAYORKAS

Question 1. According to a December 2013 GAO report, CBP and ICE continue to struggle with large portions of their TECS modernization which could result in cost overruns and delay its 2015 deployment deadline. TECS is critical to the Department's border security and law enforcement missions. Describe the management direction you are providing this project and please give the committee an update on the TECS modernization efforts and whether or not ICE and CBP will deliver its planned functionality by 2015 as originally scheduled.

Answer. DHS has a tiered governance structure that includes oversight at the senior leadership level, the component level, and the program level. At the highest level, the Department is actively monitoring both programs by way of Executive Steering Committee (ESC) meetings made up of senior-level executives, including Headquarters and Component Chief Information Officers, Chief Acquisition Executives, and Chief Financial Officers. Executive Steering Committees are decision-making bodies that provide governance and oversight for all of the Department's IT Major investments.

Currently, due to the program's high risk, the U.S. Immigration and Customs Enforcement (ICE) TECS Modernization has a monthly ESC meeting and bi-weekly deep-dive meetings with the Department's Chief Information Officer and management acquisition team. The U.S. Customs and Border Protection (CBP) TECS Modernization has bi-monthly ESC meetings.

The CBP TECS Modernization has been deploying modernized functionality incrementally since 2009 and is on track to deliver the majority of modernized capability by September 2015, as originally planned. This program has multiple releases of which 80% have been delivered. The remaining 20% will be delivered on schedule by September 2015.

The ICE TECS Modernization is in the technical evaluation phase of procuring an application vendor, with an anticipated award in September 2014. The program is currently a high-risk program due to its schedule and cost risks. Mitigation plans are in place to address the program risks. The program meets regularly with Headquarters leadership to review status and progress toward milestone events. The program is engaged with the CBP parallel effort to execute the coordinated strategy for both agencies to obtain mainframe independence from the shared legacy TECS system.

Question 2a. Does DHS believe that they are full partners in the FirstNet effort?

Answer. Yes, DHS is a full partner and one of three permanent board members in the FirstNet effort. The Department appreciates the importance of the FirstNet network to the overall security and resilience of our Nation's public safety communications infrastructure.

Question 2b. What is DHS doing to support FirstNet?

Answer. DHS is taking an active role in supporting FirstNet by providing the following products and services:

- *FirstNet Consultation Preparation Workshops.*—DHS has delivered on-site workshops in 54 of 56 States/Territories to help prepare for the FirstNet consultation process. The remaining two States/Territories will be completed this year.
- *Broadband Tools.*—DHS has developed a mobile data survey tool to help States determine the current use of commercial and private data systems within their jurisdiction that is being leveraged by FirstNet.
- *FirstNet Coordination.*—In early 2013, FirstNet asked DHS to participate with the National Telecommunications and Information Administration and FirstNet staff to coordinate outreach and data collection with public safety efforts. Since that time, DHS has participated in weekly calls, as well as periodic strategic planning meetings with FirstNet Board members and staff.

- *Federal Broadband Coordination.*—The Emergency Communications Prepared-ness Center, which is a DHS-led Federal coordination committee to improve emergency communications interoperability, has been leveraged by FirstNet for Federal outreach and planning.
- *Tribal Coordination.*—DHS provided Tribal subject matter expertise to assist FirstNet in establishing its Tribal Working Group, as well as facilitating meet-ings with key Tribal representatives.
- *Cyber and Physical Risk Assessment.*—DHS identified possible threats to and vulnerabilities of cyber infrastructure in the Nation-wide Public Safety Broadband Network that could threaten the network's reliability and security.
- *Public Safety Broadband Requirements.*—DHS helped develop first responders requirements for the Nation-wide public safety broadband network.
- *700 MHz Demonstration Network.*—DHS helped create a 700 MHz Demonstra-tion Network at the National Institute for Standards and Technology Boulder Labs to assist with performance, conformance, and interoperability testing of in-frastructure, devices, and applications. This public safety demonstration net-work and environment for testing allows public safety to better understand the new capabilities and challenges created by broadband technologies.
- *Modeling and Analysis for Public Safety Broadband.*—DHS is conducting mod-eling and simulation research on the deployment of a Nation-wide public safety broadband network. This research will provide FirstNet with insight needed to make more informed procurement-related decisions.

Question 3. The Office of Program Accountability and Risk Management (PARM) is responsible for DHS' overall acquisition management across the Department, and has work under way to implement an Acquisition Life-Cycle framework for major acquisitions. Among other things, this framework outlines key decision events over the life of a program. This "waterfall" approach may be fine for most types of acqui-sitions; but for IT acquisitions, it promotes longer time frames for delivering capa-bilities (often 5–7 years) and increased risk of cost, schedule, and performance issues. The Office of the Chief Information Officer (OCIO) is responsible for IT in-vestment governance, including IT systems development. OCIO has work under way to modify, finalize, and implement systems acquisition policies and processes in line with an incremental development approach, which calls for breaking programs into smaller increments and delivering capabilities in 6–12 month releases. It will be im-portant for PARM and OCIO to collaborate on a way forward to define roles and responsibilities, and modify the Acquisition Framework as needed to accommodate an incremental development approach to IT. How efficiently and effectively do DHS's acquisition and IT governance processes work in concert with one another to ensure that major IT investments are delivered within cost and schedule, and meet mission needs?

Answer. DHS's integrated acquisition and IT governance processes work together in an efficient and effective manner. Management Directive 102–01 establishes the Department's acquisition governance framework for both IT and non-IT programs. The Management Directorate's Office of Program Accountability and Risk Manage-ment coordinates effective integration and collaboration across the Department's lines of business, including the Office of the Chief Information Officer, to implement acquisition oversight.

Further, the Secretary's "Strengthening Unity of Effort" initiative is enhancing the coordination of Departmental planning, programming, budgeting, and execution processes through strengthened requirements processes and decision-making.

Question 4a. Component agencies of DHS are increasingly using the Government Printing Office (GPO) for the production of secure credentials. Some have expressed concern that component agencies are inappropriately using Title 44 of the United States Code as a means to enter into sole-source agreements with GPO to cir-cumvent the normal fair and open competitive procurement process.

Is there any formal or informal guidance from DHS to component agencies on the use of the GPO versus open competition?

Answer. DHS follows the requirements of Federal Acquisition Regulation 8.802, which requires printing to be done by or through GPO unless an exception applies. DHS utilizes a form (DHS 500–7) for its components to use to obtain printing serv-ices through the designated central printing authority or to seek a waiver. There is no additional acquisition guidance regarding printing.

Question 4b. What is the opinion of DHS Office of General Counsel on Title 44 of the United States Code and FAR 48 Subpart 8.8 as it relates to public printing services and use of GPO for secure credentials?

Answer. The Department recognizes the statutory and regulatory requirements related to the Government Printing Office.

Question 4c. What risk/security analysis has been done to make sure that secure credentials being used by DHS are durable, secure, and virtually counterfeit-proof?

Answer. A risk/security analysis of the secure credentials used by DHS was conducted by the General Services Administration (GSA), as the executive agent for acquisition of Homeland Security Presidential Directive—12 products and services. GSA ensures that secure credentials meet the standards of the National Institute of Standards and Technology (NIST).

To further deter counterfeiting of the secure credentials being used by DHS, the Department has gone beyond the NIST requirements by requiring visual security features with micro-text bands, the use of transparent and gradient effects, optically variable ink, and holographic images in the security laminate.

Question 4d. What alternatives analysis or analysis of alternatives (including cost and security analysis) has been done to support secure credential programs?

Answer. During an analysis of alternatives conducted by the DHS Office of the Chief Security Officer, it was determined that GPO met standards for secure credentials. GPO delivered added value with strict adherence to a secure Government supply chain requirement and smart card product manufacturing. GPO also demonstrated oversight of security in the transportation of raw materials and finished goods, and the physical security of the card manufacturer's plant and information technology systems.

Question 4e. How much has DHS obligated and expended in fiscal year 2010–fiscal year 2013 for secure credentials printed by GPO? How much does DHS plan to spend on secure credentials in fiscal year 2014?

Answer. DHS has obligated and expended a total of $7,494,875 between fiscal year 2010–fiscal year 2013. The breakdown per fiscal year is as follows:

Fiscal year 2010: $1,769,962.00
Fiscal year 2011: $1,891,963.00
Fiscal year 2012: $2,432,350.00
Fiscal year 2013: $1,400,600.00
Fiscal year 2014 Plan: $2,491,125.00.

Question 5a. According to news reports from early April, top hiring officials at CBP broke Federal civil service laws when they tried to hire three politically connected but unqualified candidates who were favored by the agency's then-commissioner Alan Bersin. Shortly before arriving at CBP, Mr. Bersin allegedly gave the human resources staff three names and told them he wanted to hire the individuals as political appointees. However, the slots for those jobs, known as Schedule C positions, were filled. The staff then attempted to hire them into open civil service positions at the GS–13 level, as management and policy analysts.

Who were the people seeking career positions in these reported cases? Are they employed by CBP currently? If so, under what hiring authorities?

Answer. The Office of Special Counsel (OSC) has released a press statement regarding its complaint for disciplinary action before the Merit Systems Protection Board (MSPB), filed against Katherine Coffman. The OSC has not yet made the complaint a public document and DHS is not a party to the litigation. Further, in accordance with DHS practice, and per OSC preference, DHS does not comment on pending litigation. DHS does not wish to impede the current adjudication of this case by releasing specific information relevant to the MSPB proceeding, or by providing opinions regarding any specific allegations or evidence that may be contained within the complaint as described in the public press statement. Therefore, in this and subsequent responses, DHS will only answer as to matters not at issue in the litigation.

Question 5b. Who within the DHS Office of the Chief Human Capital Officer rejected most of the career conversion requests and approved the one OPM later rejected? Please provide necessary documents asking for and rejecting these personnel actions.

Answer. Please see above.

Question 5c. Since Ms. Katherine Coffman is in the position to hire individuals across CBP, does she assert inappropriate influence over the career civil service hiring process? Did she or does she seek to hire others who fit "political criteria" favored by her or Mr. Bersin?

Answer. Please see above.

Question 5d. What was the role of the Office of the White House Liaison at DHS in these career conversions? Is the Office of the White House Liaison involved in interviewing or vetting other career candidates for Federal employment?

Answer. DHS has inquired of the relevant individuals and reviewed the relevant files and has no reason to believe the Office of the White House Liaison was involved in the attempted conversion from political appointments to career appointments for the three individuals whom it is alleged Mr. Bersin wanted to hire at CBP.

I am informed it is not.

Question 5e. Since January 21, 2009, how many political appointees have been converted to career employees? If any, please identify them along with their titles and the office in which they are working.

Answer. Prior to January 2010, Federal agencies had to seek OPM's approval of conversions to competitive service positions only during Presidential election years. As a result, DHS did not maintain DHS-wide records specific to such conversions and cannot readily access this information for the time period between January 21, 2009 and December 31, 2009.

Beginning on January 1, 2010, OPM required agencies to seek prior approval from OPM before appointing a current or recent political appointee to a competitive or non-political excepted service position at any level under the provisions of title 5, United States Code. OPM provided DHS with information based on OPM's records which establish that since January 2009, six political appointees have been converted to career positions.

In 2009, an individual was appointed to a GS–14 policy analyst position in the Office of Civil Rights & Civil Liberties. In 2011, an individual was appointed to a Senior Executive Service position in the Office of Science and Technology. In 2012, an individual was appointed to a Senior Executive Service position in the Federal Emergency Management Agency and another individual was appointed to a GS–13 external affairs specialist position, also in FEMA. In 2013, two individuals were appointed to two different Senior Executive Services positions; one in the United States Coast Guard and another in the Office of the General Counsel.

Question 5f. Given the allegations in this matter, do you have confidence in Mr. Bersin as a senior leader of DHS? Have you considered putting Mr. Bersin or Ms. Coffman on administrative leave while these allegations are fully investigated by the Office of Special Counsel and the Merit Systems Protections Board?

Answer. Yes, the leadership of the Department has full confidence in Mr. Bersin. Neither the Office of the Special Counsel (OSC) nor the Merit Systems Protection Board (MSPB) has suggested such an action, and DHS has determined not to take such action at this time.

The current posture of the proceedings is that the OSC has completed its investigation and filed complaints seeking disciplinary action against three CBP career officials. The MSPB has jurisdiction over the complaints. DHS is not aware that OSC or the MSPB will conduct any further investigation.

QUESTION FROM HONORABLE PATRICK MEEHAN FOR ALEJANDRO N. MAYORKAS

Question. I submitted a question for the record following Secretary Johnson's first appearance before the committee that remains unanswered regarding EAGLE II, an information technology multiple-award contract vehicle potentially worth $22 billion over 5 to 7 years. It is my understanding that companies were notified of additional awards being made in early May on highly protested functional category one of the vehicle. The announcement appears to cut both ways—more vendors means more competition, but also more proposals to evaluate thus slowing down the acquisition selection process.

What information have you received about this procurement and what is your impression of how this acquisition was conducted? How is DHS going to make sure that programs actually use this vehicle and that proposals received per task order will be evaluated in a timely manner?

Answer. As Deputy Secretary, I was not personally involved in this procurement and therefore have only had access to publicly-available information in accordance with Federal regulation. I have been made aware of the award information and am informed that the procurement was conducted in an open and transparent manner, employing Federal procurement best practices and in accordance with the Federal Acquisition Regulation. Like its predecessor, EAGLE II attracted significant interest from industry.

I am further informed that, since the EAGLE II competition received a robust industry response, completing a fair and detailed evaluation of each of the proposals required a significant amount of time and resources. Protests are part of the procurement process for these large competitions. The DHS personnel responsible for the EAGLE II procurement participated transparently and professionally in the protest process to ensure all companies had an opportunity to have their concerns addressed in an impartial forum.

To date, several protests have been dismissed and contract awards have been made to large, small, service-disabled veteran-owned, HUBZone, and 8(a) American companies. Task orders have already been placed by several DHS components. Task Order awards to date include 18 awards made to various small business totaling $16.5 million with a total value of $63.8 million if all option periods are exercised.

The Office of the Chief Procurement Officer is monitoring EAGLE II spending. DHS continues to increase its use of strategic sourcing vehicles such as EAGLE II because they provide a streamlined and efficient process for obtaining services and result in cost savings for the programs. It is the Department's policy that the EAGLE II contracts be used unless there is an alternative that will yield a lower price or better support the DHS small business program.

To streamline task order competitions and evaluations, DHS offers training on the use of EAGLE II for all components and has generated an ordering guide that includes guidance, templates, and points of contact for users. This guidance ensures that task order proposals are evaluated promptly and accurately. DHS has a task order ombudsman available to assist any EAGLE II contractor that becomes concerned that a task order proposal evaluation has been delayed.

QUESTIONS FROM HONORABLE TOM MARINO FOR ALEJANDRO N. MAYORKAS

Question 1a. What percentage of NFIP claims from Superstorm Sandy contained fraudulent losses? Can you quantify that with a dollar amount?

Answer. FEMA takes seriously its responsibility to be a good steward of Federal funds, which include not only tax dollars but also flood insurance premiums. Reducing, investigating, and ultimately eliminating waste, fraud, and abuse is an important part of that responsibility. When FEMA becomes aware of evidence of potential fraud on the part of NFIP policyholders, building repair contractors, or others, the FEMA Office of Chief Counsel and the Office of the Chief Security Officer's FEMA Fraud Unit work with the Office of the Inspector General to investigate. While the FEMA Fraud Unit and the Office of the Inspector General work closely in developing cases, FEMA is typically not informed of results as a matter of practice, since the issue at hand may be a criminal matter.

While legally distinct from fraud, FEMA also tracks improper payments pursuant to the Improper Payments Act. The tracking does not differentiate underpayments, overpayments, or fraud. The results are as follows:

Fiscal Year	Improper Payment Rate
2008	6.38%
2009	2.22%
2010	1.21%
2011	0.75%
2012	0.02%

No, for the same reason explained in the answer above: FEMA is typically not informed of investigative results as a matter of practice, since the issue at hand may be a criminal matter.

Question 1b. What is the policy for ensuring that claims are legitimate before releasing funds for rebuilding?

Answer. There are a number of checks involved in the claims handling process. After a claim is filed, the NFIP insurer assigns an independent adjuster, who is certified as an NFIP adjuster and has knowledge of the coverage and exclusions under the Standard Flood Insurance Policy. The independent adjuster will inspect the insured property, preferably together with the insured to validate that the adjuster reviews all of the components of the property that the insured believes had been damaged by flood. The adjuster describes the claim process to the policyholder and provides a copy of the NFIP Flood Insurance Claims Handbook, which is a tool developed by FEMA to explain the claims process to policyholders after a loss. During this inspection, the adjuster measures, photographs, and notes elements of flood damage. The adjuster then prepares a detailed room-by-room, line-by-line estimate of the damage caused by flood. A report documenting the observed damage is then provided for review by the insurer, which is responsible for identifying covered losses and making payment. Unless there is an express written waiver, within 60 days after the loss the insured is required to provide a proof of loss, which is the insured's sworn statement of the amount being claimed.

Question 1c. Additionally, what tools does the agency have to "claw-back" funds released to homeowners who submitted fraudulent claims?

Answer. All forms of the Standard Flood Insurance Policy ("SFIP") have provisions governing improper activities by the insured and void the policy in the event of fraud or misrepresentation. If the policy is void, the NFIP is authorized to recoup payments and can do so through a Debt Collection action or affirmative litigation. In addition, the United States has available civil and criminal remedies, including the False Claims Act, to recoup fraudulently-claimed funds and to seek civil and criminal penalties. The DHS Office of Inspector General and other Federal law enforcement, including a FEMA Fraud unit, are available to investigate allegations of fraud, and FEMA also will work with State and local law enforcement in appropriate circumstances to investigate and prosecute fraud.

Question 2. DHS is over 10 years old and it seems that we are only now getting to understand what a "high-risk" program is. This is unacceptably long. What took so long and what assurances can you give that we won't have more oversight failures going forward?

Answer. DHS has a clear understanding of its "high-risk" programs, as defined on a biennial basis by the Government Accountability Office (GAO) through publication of its GAO High-Risk List. We work closely with GAO to address the areas where DHS remains on the High-Risk List. When I became deputy secretary of DHS in late December 2013, the first action I took was to schedule a meeting with GAO Comptroller General Dodaro. DHS and GAO meet regularly to discuss progress on our High-Risk designation, and I have been able to participate in several of those productive meetings.

In 2011, DHS published the *Integrated Strategy for High-Risk Management* (Strategy), to address our High-Risk designation. DHS continues to make progress towards High-Risk List removal and publishes an updated Strategy on a semi-annual basis. Of note is the fact that GAO has stated in its most recent High-Risk List update that our Department's Strategy, "if implemented and sustained, provides a path for DHS to be removed from GAO's High-Risk List." Further, earlier this year we developed specific action plans to address the 30 key outcomes GAO identified as part of the management High-Risk area. Our action plans provide month-to-month goals that offer a road map to success. Our development of these action plans provided us with the opportunity to freshly review our previous efforts and, in certain critical areas, to accelerate our time tables materially.

Question 3. Many of the DHS operating agencies like CBP, TSA, and the Coast Guard came with internal inspection capabilities when DHS was created. Yet it appears the senior levels have been slow to organize Department-wide oversight. It appears that these agencies are not a "part of the whole" from the management perspective. When will DHS-wide management controls be in place?

Answer. To further Department-wide management integration, Secretary Johnson directed the "Strengthening Departmental Unity of Effort" initiative in April 2014. In this initiative, the Secretary directs specific activities across four main lines of effort: Inclusive senior leader discussion and decision-making forums that provide an environment of trust and transparency; strengthened management processes for investment, including requirements, budget, and acquisition processes, that look at cross-cutting issues across the Department; focused, collaborative Departmental strategy, planning, and analytic capability that supports more effective DHS-wide decision-making and operations; and enhanced coordinated operations to harness the significant resources of the Department more effectively. The goal is better understanding of the broad and complex DHS mission space and empowering DHS components to effectively execute their operations.

To that end, the Secretary, in a June 26, 2014 memorandum to DHS leadership, established the DHS Joint Requirements Council to "look at cross-component requirements and develop recommendations for investment, as well as changes to training organization, laws, and operational processes and procedures." This component-led, component-driven body will be organized around the five DHS primary mission areas and begin to tackle issues involving information-based screening and vetting; chemical, biological, radiological, and nuclear surveillance and detection; aviation commonality; cybersecurity; and information sharing with potential impacts beginning as early as the DHS budget submission to OMB this September. Other unity-of-effort initiative pieces, including strengthened budget and acquisition process, will also lead to greater management control.

Question 4. Referring to your technology programs across DHS, there is strong criticism from the private-sector suppliers that DHS fails to provide multi-year plans that would guide private R&D investment. Why can't DHS seem to get forward planning for major programs right?

Answer. A primary challenge in developing and executing optimal multi-year plans to guide private R&D investment is the reality of fiscal uncertainty: The Department is not assured of sustained funding streams for long-term efforts.

DHS has worked hard to create a sustainable process to validate Department-wide requirements across the DHS primary mission areas to inform investment decisions and drive acquisitions. The Secretary's June 26, 2014 memorandum to DHS leadership establishing a DHS Joint Requirements Council to "look at cross-component requirements and develop recommendations for investment, as well as changes to training organization, laws, and operational processes and procedures" will help us to achieve that goal. By studying requirements across components and developing "joint" solutions from a range of potential alternative capabilities, the Department should be able to more predictably interface with the private sector earlier in order to better partner to meet the challenges faced by the Nation in securing the homeland.

Further, the Department's increased focus on looking at full life-cycle program costs across the entire 5-year Homeland Security budget should increase awareness and reduce uncertainty for our private industry partners. To this end, newly-confirmed Under Secretary for Science and Technology Dr. Reginald Brothers has also prioritized development of an updated Science and Technology Directorate (S&T) Strategic Plan complemented by technology roadmaps in S&T's major investment areas. These types of products are fundamental for communicating S&T's direction and vision to industry in order to better align and incentivize private R&D investment in DHS and Homeland Security Enterprise needs and priorities. Moving forward, S&T's Strategic Plan and roadmaps, along with a revamped approach to creating and sharing project requirements, will help strengthen and energize the Department's and S&T's partnership with the Homeland Security Industrial Base.

QUESTION FROM CHAIRMAN MICHAEL T. MCCAUL AND RANKING MEMBER BENNIE G. THOMPSON FOR GENE L. DODARO

Question. Please provide us in writing what you think it would take for the Department of Homeland Security (DHS) to run seamlessly, all the components within the Department using one standard for procurement and other things.

Answer. DHS could enhance its overall efficiency and effectiveness by continuing to implement and strengthen key management initiatives, including fully achieving key management outcomes that we and DHS have agreed are necessary for addressing our designation of DHS management functions as high-risk. Achieving some of these outcomes will entail implementing Department-wide standards, such as standards pertaining to information technology (IT) and acquisition management.

Specifically, DHS needs to demonstrate continued progress in implementing and strengthening key management initiatives and addressing corrective actions and outcomes in human capital management, acquisition management, financial management, and IT. This includes taking steps to implement certain common standards Department-wide. For example,

- As we reported in May 2014, DHS's acquisition policy largely reflects key acquisition management practices, but the Department has not implemented the policy consistently.[1] For example, in March 2014, we found that the Transportation Security Administration (TSA) does not collect or analyze available information that could be used to enhance the effectiveness of its advanced imaging technology.[2] In March 2014, we also found that U.S. Customs and Border Protection (CBP) had not fully followed DHS policy regarding testing for the integrated fixed towers being deployed on the Arizona border.[3] We recommended that CBP revise its testing plan in accordance with DHS acquisition guidance, among other things. DHS did not concur with our recommendation and stated that the existing test plan will provide much, if not all, of the insight contemplated by the intent of the recommendation. We continue to believe that revising the test plan to include more robust testing to determine operational effectiveness and suitability could better position CBP to evaluate integrated fixed-tower capabilities before moving to full production for the system, help provide CBP with information on the extent to which the towers satisfy the Border Patrol's user requirements, and help reduce potential program risks.
- In May 2014, we also reported that work is needed to demonstrate progress in implementing IT investment management processes across DHS's 13 IT invest-

---

[1] GAO, *Department of Homeland Security: Progress Made; Significant Work Remains in Addressing High-Risk Areas,* GAO–14–532T (Washington, DC: May 7, 2014).

[2] GAO, *Advanced Imaging Technology: TSA Needs Additional Information Before Procuring Next-Generation Systems,* GAO–14–357 (Washington, DC: Mar. 31, 2014).

[3] GAO, *Arizona Border Surveillance Technology Plan: Additional Actions Needed to Strengthen Management and Assess Effectiveness,* GAO–14–368 (Washington, DC: Mar. 3, 2014). Integrated fixed towers are to consist of surveillance equipment (for example, ground surveillance radars and surveillance cameras) mounted on fixed, that is, stationary towers, and power generation and communication equipment to support the towers.

ment portfolios.[4] In July 2012, we recommended that DHS finalize the policies and procedures associated with its new tiered IT governance structure and continue to implement key processes supporting this structure.[5] DHS agreed with these recommendations; however, as of April 2014, the Department had not finalized the key IT governance directive, and the draft structure had been implemented across only 5 of the 13 investment portfolios.[6]

More uniformly implementing these common standards across the Department and showing measurable, sustainable progress in implementing other key management initiatives can help DHS more fully address GAO's high-risk designation. We are continuing to review DHS's progress in these areas and will update our assessment of DHS's efforts to address our high-risk designation early next year.

QUESTION FROM HONORABLE YVETTE D. CLARKE FOR GENE L. DODARO

Question. Some individuals believe that DHS disciplinary practices are inequitable and oftentimes arbitrary. For example, there is no Department-wide standard for penalties, and the same offense can engender different results without any sound reason for this discrepancy. Would you agree that the Department could benefit from standardized disciplinary processes? Does not having these processes in place have an impact on low morale, for instance? If not, why?

Answer. We have not specifically assessed the standardization of disciplinary practices at DHS, but our work has found that TSA could strengthen its monitoring of allegations of employee misconduct.

In July 2013, we found that TSA could strengthen its monitoring of allegations of employee misconduct.[7] Specifically, we found that:

- According to TSA employee misconduct data that we analyzed, TSA investigated and adjudicated approximately 9,600 cases of employee misconduct from fiscal years 2010 through 2012. While TSA had taken steps to help manage the investigations and adjudication process, such as providing training to TSA staff at airports, we found that additional procedures could help TSA better monitor the investigations and adjudications process. For example, TSA did not have a process for conducting reviews of misconduct cases to verify that TSA staff at airports were complying with policies and procedures for adjudicating employee misconduct. We concluded that without a review process, it is difficult to determine the extent to which deficiencies, if any, exist in the adjudications process.

- Further, we found that TSA did not record all misconduct case outcomes, including outcomes in cases that resulted in corrective action or no penalty, in its centralized case management system because the agency had not issued guidance requiring the recording of all outcomes. We concluded that issuing guidance to TSA staff at airports about recording all case outcomes in the database would emphasize management's view of the importance of staff including such information to provide a more complete record of adjudication decisions.

- We recommended, among other things, that TSA establish a process to conduct reviews of misconduct cases to verify that TSA staff at airports are complying with policies and procedures for adjudicating employee misconduct, and develop and issue guidance to the field clarifying the need for TSA officials at airports to record all misconduct case outcomes in the centralized case management system. DHS concurred with the recommendations, and TSA is taking actions in response, such as increased auditing of disciplinary records to help ensure that airport staff are complying with policies and procedures for adjudicating employee misconduct.

QUESTION FROM CHAIRMAN MICHAEL T. MCCAUL FOR GENE L. DODARO

Question. Please elaborate on your comments regarding Congressional committees with a jurisdiction on homeland security issues. Specifically, to what extent have repetitive or redundant hearings and briefings (i.e., those involving substantially the same subject matter but provided separately to more than one committee) led to inefficiencies and inhibited progress by the Department to address items on the High-Risk List? Have these particular hearings and briefings increased over time, in com-

---

[4] GAO–14–532T.

[5] GAO, *Information Technology: DHS Needs to Further Define and Implement Its New Governance Process*, GAO–12–818 (Washington, DC: July 25, 2012).

[6] The draft structure had been implemented across the following five portfolios: Intelligence, screening, information sharing and safeguarding, enterprise IT services, and enterprise human capital.

[7] GAO, *Transportation Security: TSA Could Strengthen Monitoring of Allegations of Employee Misconduct*, GAO–13–624 (Washington, DC: July 30, 2013).

parison to previous Congresses? Does the fact that multiple components at the Department lacking authorizations (which have not been enacted due to jurisdictional battles) have any effect on the ability of these components and DHS Headquarters to enact necessary reforms, since potential necessary authorities are not codified?

Answer. GAO has not analyzed the impact of hearings and briefings on DHS's ability to address items on GAO's high-risk list, trends in the number of DHS-related hearings and briefings, or the potential effects of the lack of authorizing legislation on DHS's ability to carry out necessary reforms. In December 2002, we did report that the creation of DHS had raised questions regarding how the Congress could best meet its oversight responsibilities, and that DHS would be overseen by numerous Congressional committees.[8] At the time we observed that the Congress may wish to explore ways to facilitate conducting its responsibilities in a more consolidated and integrated manner, and noted that whether the Congress did so could have an impact on the effective implementation and oversight of DHS.

In 2003 we designated implementing and transforming the Department of Homeland Security as high-risk because DHS had to transform 22 agencies—several with major management challenges—into one department, and failure to address associated risks could have serious consequences for U.S. National and economic security.[9] It is noteworthy to recognize, however, that since 2003, DHS has made considerable progress in transforming its original component agencies into a single department. As a result, in our 2013 high-risk update, we narrowed the scope of the high-risk area to focus on strengthening DHS management functions.[10]

DHS remains on the high-risk list because the Department has not made sufficient progress addressing GAO's high-risk removal criteria, such as having a framework to monitor progress, capacity (having sufficient resources), and demonstrating clear, sustained progress. Specifically, our work at DHS has found that the Department has made progress strengthening its management functions, including developing policies that provide a framework for addressing management challenges. However, we have found in our past work that DHS does not always adhere to its own policies. For example, DHS's acquisition policy largely reflects key acquisition management practices, but in September 2012, we found that the Department has not implemented the practices consistently. Further, we found that DHS has made progress in initiating efforts to validate required acquisition documents.[11] However, the Department does not have the acquisition management tools in place to consistently demonstrate whether its major acquisition programs are on track to achieve their cost, schedule, and capability goals. Accordingly, about half of DHS's major programs lack an approved baseline, and 77 percent lack approved life-cycle cost estimates.

QUESTION FROM HONORABLE JEFF DUNCAN FOR GENE L. DODARO

Question. The Office of Program Accountability and Risk Management (PARM) is responsible for DHS's overall acquisition management across the Department, and has work underway to implement an Acquisition Life Cycle framework for major acquisitions. Among other things, this framework outlines key decision events over the life of a program. This "waterfall" approach may be fine for most types of acquisitions; but for IT acquisitions, it promotes longer time frames for delivering capabilities (often 5–7 years) and increased risk of cost, schedule, and performance issues. The Office of the Chief Information Officer (OCIO) is responsible for IT investment governance, including IT systems development. OCIO has work underway to modify, finalize, and implement systems acquisition policies and processes in line with an incremental development approach, which calls for breaking programs into smaller increments and delivering capabilities in 6–12 month releases. It will be important for PARM and OCIO to collaborate on a way forward to define roles and responsibilities, and modify the Acquisition Framework as needed to accommodate an incremental development approach to IT. How efficiently and effectively do DHS's acquisition and IT governance processes work in concert with one another to ensure that major IT investments are delivered within cost and schedule, and meet mission needs?

Answer. We have found in our prior work that DHS has not yet fully established or finalized its acquisition and IT governance processes; however, we found that

---

[8] GAO, *Homeland Security: Management Challenges Facing Federal Leadership,* GAO–03–260 (Washington, DC: Dec. 20, 2002).

[9] GAO, *High-Risk Series: An Update,* GAO–03–119 (Washington, DC: Jan. 1, 2003).

[10] GAO, *High-Risk Series: An Update,* GAO–13–283 (Washington, DC: Feb. 14, 2013).

[11] GAO, *Homeland Security: DHS Requires More Disciplined Investment Management to Help Meet Mission Needs,* GAO–12–833 (Washington, DC: Sept. 18, 2012).

these processes, as defined and implemented thus far, may be leading to slowed IT development work, as well as ineffective or redundant executive oversight reviews. For example:

- *Slowed IT development work.*—In our May 2014 report on agencies' IT incremental development policies and approaches, we found that DHS OCIO officials had cited inefficient governance and oversight processes as one common factor, among others, inhibiting incremental development during a 6-month period.[12] To illustrate, those officials said that it can take up to 2 months to schedule a meeting with DHS review boards prior to releasing functionality. However, we also reported that a Program Accountability and Risk Management (PARM) official disagreed with that statement, maintaining that DHS's acquisition review boards perform reviews very quickly, and that any delays in completing these reviews are attributable to investments being unprepared. Further, DHS OCIO officials suggested that oversight of programs using an Agile development methodology should be performed at the lowest practicable level of the organization.[13] Regardless of the cause, these inefficiencies are hampering DHS's ability to deploy IT capabilities in 6-month increments. Accordingly, we recommended that DHS consider factors that either enable or inhibit incremental development when updating the Department's policies governing incremental IT development. DHS concurred with our recommendation and stated that it plans to include strategies in its guidance to minimize factors identified as inhibiting incremental development. It will be important for DHS's OCIO and PARM offices to work collaboratively to effectively address this recommendation.

- *Ineffective or redundant executive oversight reviews.*—In December 2013, we reported on the effectiveness of the executive governance and oversight of the Department's two TECS modernization (TECS Mod) border security programs.[14] While we found that OCIO and PARM had taken actions to oversee the two programs, the lack of complete, timely, and accurate data had affected their ability to make informed and timely decisions, thus limiting their effectiveness in several cases. For example, we found that OCIO had rated one of the programs as moderately low-risk in its most recent program health assessment, based partially on U.S. Customs and Border Protection's use of earned value management. However, the program manager told us that the other program was not using this management technique. In addition, PARM had rated the other program as low-risk in its most recent Quarterly Program Accountability Report based in part on outdated cost and schedule estimates. Accordingly, we made a recommendation to improve the data used by these governing bodies for major IT acquisition programs. DHS concurred and stated that it has taken steps to ensure that the data used by the IT program acquisition programs are accurate and complete, such as implementing a decision support tool. However, we identified instances where DHS governance and oversight bodies were acting on information that was not complete, timely, or accurate, despite the presence of such a tool.

  In addition, while both PARM and OCIO have responsibility for ensuring that IT system acquisition programs are on track, it is not always clear whether these roles are distinct. Our December 2013 review also showed overlap in the program assessments conducted by PARM and OCIO—in particular, with regard to risk and requirements management, and cost and schedule performance. We recently initiated a review to, among other things, assess PARM's coordination efforts with DHS components (including OCIO) to conduct oversight of major acquisitions.

Additionally, as we testified in May 2014, the Department has yet to finalize its key IT governance directive, and the draft structure has been implemented across only 5 of the 13 IT investment portfolios.[15] It will be critical for DHS to complete

---

[12] GAO, *Information Technology: Agencies Need to Establish and Implement Incremental Development Policies*, GAO–14–361 (Washington, DC: May 1, 2014).

[13] Agile development calls for the delivery of software in small, short increments rather than in the typically long, sequential phases of a traditional waterfall approach. More a philosophy than a methodology, Agile emphasizes early and continuous software delivery, as well as using collaborative teams and measuring progress with working software. The Agile approach was first articulated in a 2001 document called the Agile Manifesto, which is still used today. The manifesto has four values: (1) Individuals and interactions over processes and tools, (2) working software over comprehensive documentation, (3) customer collaboration over contract negotiation, and (4) responding to change over following a plan.

[14] GAO, *Border Security: DHS's Efforts to Modernize Key Enforcement Systems Could Be Strengthened*, GAO–14–62 (Washington, DC: Dec. 5, 2013).

[15] GAO, *Department of Homeland Security: Progress Made; Significant Work Remains in Addressing High-Risk Areas*, GAO–14–532T (Washington, DC: May 7, 2014).

these actions in order to ensure that all IT investments are appropriately aligned with the Department's enterprise architecture (i.e., to avoid acquiring duplicative or overlapping systems), adequately overseen to ensure that key IT management controls (e.g., requirements management) are being properly implemented and monitored, and delivered as planned. Because both PARM and OCIO play important roles in ensuring that IT investments are effectively acquired and implemented, these two organizations will need to work closely together to ensure that IT projects are delivered incrementally and often and that DHS finalizes the IT governance directive.

QUESTION FROM HONORABLE TOM MARINO FOR GENE L. DODARO

Question. In your testimony you mention that the National Flood Insurance Program (NFIP) has not made a single payment on the principal borrowed from the Department of the Treasury since 2010. Under current law, could you estimate when the NFIP would, or could, fully repay the amount owed to the Treasury?

Answer. We have not made our own estimates of how long the Federal Emergency Management Agency (FEMA) would need to repay the $24 billion it has borrowed from Treasury for the NFIP. Nevertheless, information from a report we issued in April 2014 provides some insight into FEMA's prospects for repayment.[16] In that report, we noted that the Biggert-Waters Flood Insurance Reform Act of 2012 (Biggert-Waters Act) requires FEMA to issue a report to Congress setting forth options to repay FEMA's total debt to Treasury within 10 years.[17] Although the report was due in January 2013, FEMA has not yet issued such a report. FEMA officials told us that before the enactment of the Homeowner Flood Insurance Affordability Act of 2014 (2014 Act), they had conducted preliminary analysis assessing FEMA's repayment ability under scenarios that use different assumptions about future NFIP losses.[18] The officials said the assessment showed that, under FEMA's planned implementation of the Biggert-Waters Act, the agency would not reach the 10-year repayment goal under any of the scenarios. Implementation of the 2014 Act may further reduce the likelihood of repayment within 10 years because the Act reduces future program premium revenue by reinstating subsidized and grandfathered rates the Biggert-Waters Act had eliminated.

Our April 2014 report also noted that, according to FEMA officials, in some years the agency has not had sufficient funds to make principal payments and, in other years, could have made principal payments but chose to preserve its cash balances to help avoid the need for future borrowing. A key factor affecting FEMA's future borrowing needs and ability to repay its debt is future losses. However, the frequency and severity of future flood losses are difficult to predict.

QUESTIONS FROM CHAIRMAN MICHAEL T. MCCAUL FOR JOHN ROTH

Question 1. In your testimony, you highlighted a November 2012 audit where the Department of Homeland Security (DHS) Office of Inspector General (OIG) tested DHS radios to determine whether DHS components could talk to each other in the event of a terrorist event or other emergency. Only 1 of 479 radio users tested— or less than one-quarter of 1 percent—could access and use the specified common channel to communicate. Further, of the 382 radios tested, only 20 percent (78) contained all the correct program settings for the common channel. You testified that the reason the response rate was so low was that DHS did not establish an effective governing structure with the authority and responsibility to ensure it achieved Department-wide, interoperable radio communications. What is needed for DHS to establish an effective governing structure to solve this problem? What progress has DHS made since the report in ensuring operators know how to properly use their radio?

Answer. According to the Office of Management and Budget, an effective governing structure includes clearly-defined areas of responsibility, appropriately delegated authority, and a suitable hierarchy for reporting. DHS created working groups, committees, and offices to explore Department-wide communication issues, including interoperability. However, none had the authority to implement and enforce their recommendations. DHS must establish a structure that has actual authority to enforce recommendations.

DHS prepared a draft DHS Communications Interoperability Plan (DCIP). As of today, the DCIP is still in draft. According to the DCIP, as we pointed out in our

---

[16] GAO, *Economic Development: Overview of GAO's Past Work on the National Flood Insurance Program,* GAO–14–297R (Washington, DC: Apr. 9, 2014).

[17] Pub. L. No. 112–141, § 100213(b), 126 Stat. 405, 924.

[18] See Pub. L. No. 113–89, 128 Stat. 1020.

report, governance is the critical foundation of all efforts to address communication interoperability. Also according to the DCIP, existing agreements governing interoperability do not sufficiently support DHS' current needs. The Joint Wireless Program Management Office (JWPMO) and the One DHS Emergency Communications Committee are coordinating to determine appropriate roles and responsibilities. According to DHS, on March 17, 2013, the DCIP was briefed to the One DHS Emergency Communications Committee. It was approved and signed by the Assistant Secretary for the National Protection and Programs Directorate; however, the DCIP is on hold, pending a review of the Tactical Communications Executive Steering Committee (TacCom ESC) and the outcome of H.R. 4289, the *Department of Homeland Security Interoperable Communications Act.* Wording in H.R. 4289 may lead to a redefinition of interoperability and reassignment of interoperable responsibilities. The estimated date of DCIP signature has been extended from April 14, 2014, to the end of fiscal year 2014 (September 30, 2014). This will allow time for the TacCom ESC meeting to be scheduled and completed, as well as allow time for any requested, additional follow-up briefings.

Historically, the JWPMO and its predecessor organizations have not had success in achieving interoperability.

Question 2. It appears that the technology is available to achieve interoperable communications. Does DHS have the proper infrastructure to use their IT network as a way to connect radios and other devices, such as smartphones, in both a command center and an operational environment?

Answer. DHS does not currently have the IT infrastructure to support a broadband network in the operational environment. We have not done any work specifically looking at this capability, but the available body of knowledge provides the following insights.

- A broadband network could improve incident response, by providing video and data not currently available on Land Mobile Radio (LMR) systems; Nation-wide access; and interoperability.
  - The Government Accountability Office (GAO) and public safety organizations and officials indicate that mission-critical voice communication will not likely be available on broadband networks for many years.
  - There is disagreement among industry experts about how soon mission-critical voice capability could be available—some industry experts predict voice capabilities will be available within a few years, while others project it will not be available for at least a decade.
  - Long-term Evolution (LTE), the Federal Communications Commission standard for public safety broadband communication, is not currently designed to support mission-critical voice communication, such as push-to-talk.
  - GAO has reported other communication limitations associated with broadband networks, such as limited network access inside large buildings or underground.
  - GAO has reported that any new broadband network could require up to 10 times the number of towers as current LMR systems because, as a cellular network, broadband would use a series of lower power towers to transmit signals and reduce interference.
  - Additional towers for the broadband network would also need to be hardened to withstand disasters, such as hurricanes.
  - GAO has reported that a broadband network would supplement, rather than replace, LMR systems for the foreseeable future. Also, until there is mission-critical voice communication, a public safety broadband network will not resolve interoperability issues exacerbated by past emergency responses.
- DHS approved its TacNet program in March 2011 and directed establishment of the JWPMO to coordinate the program.
  - TacNet, a new DHS acquisition program, seeks to leverage public safety broadband and commercial networks to develop a single network capable of supporting voice, video, and data capabilities through DHS subscriptions to LTE public safety and commercial broadband networks.
  - In collaboration with the JWPMO, the DHS Science & Technology Directorate plans to award $7.5 million in contracts this fiscal year for a technology demonstrator program that will offer mission-critical voice capabilities and accommodate DHS video and data needs on a broadband, LTE network.
  - DHS plans to limit upgrading and modernizing its current LMR systems, based on DHS priorities and mission-critical needs, to address equipment obsolescence, Federal narrowband and security requirements, and interoperability standards.
  - DHS has estimated that full modernization of its legacy radio systems to meet these requirements would cost about $3.2 billion. In March 2012, DHS

awarded a $3 billion Department-wide contract to acquire equipment and services needed to maintain, upgrade, and modernize its legacy LMR system.

QUESTION FROM HONORABLE JEFF DUNCAN FOR JOHN ROTH

Question. According to an AP news report in 2012, Suzanne Barr, a senior Obama administration political appointee at Immigration and Customs Enforcement (ICE), resigned amid allegations of inappropriate sexual behavior and cultivating a "frat house" atmosphere at ICE. Prior to her resignation, Suzanne Barr was serving as chief of staff to former ICE Director John Morton. It appears that an OIG investigation was started, but did not continue after Barr resigned. As the newly-confirmed DHS inspector general, please explain to the committee what became of this investigation and why it appears that the investigation did not continue.

Answer. The Office of Investigations, Office of Inspector General, did not open an investigation into allegations of misconduct by Suzanne Barr in 2012. We conducted a preliminary inquiry as we were made aware of the allegations. We established there was an on-going Title VII civil suit filed by an Immigration and Customs Enforcement special agent in charge in New York City claiming harassment and retaliation. This litigation overlapped with the allegations we were aware of. Additionally, Suzanne Barr resigned in September 2012. Any Office of Inspector General administrative investigation would have been rendered moot as she was no longer a DHS employee.

With regards to an allegation we received in November 2011, in December 2011 the Office of Inspector General issued a Report of Investigation to then-Immigration and Customs Enforcement Director John Morton. The investigation was initiated based on a referral from Immigration and Customs Enforcement, Office of Professional Responsibility alleging that Suzanne Barr and Tracey Bardoff, assistant director, Immigration and Customs Enforcement misused Government funds to pay for their July 20, 2011 official travel to Mexico City, Mexico and a subsequent personal trip to Cancún, Mexico on July 22, 2011. The allegation further stated neither attended the official meetings in Mexico City, Mexico. The investigation developed no evidence that either Barr or Bardoff misused Government funds.

○